THE NEXT WAVE

THE NEXT WAVE

ON THE HUNT FOR AL QAEDA'S AMERICAN RECRUITS

CATHERINE HERRIDGE

CROWN
FORUM

NEW YORK

Copyright © 2011 by Catherine Herridge

Published in the United States by Crown Forum,
an imprint of the Crown Publishing Group,
a division of Random House, Inc., New York.

www.crownpublishing.com

CROWN and the Crown Forum colophon are registered
trademarks of Random House, Inc.

Library of Congress Cataloging-in-Publication Data

Herridge, Catherine.
The next wave : on the hunt for al Qaeda's American recruits / Catherine
Herridge.—1st ed.
p.   cm.
Includes bibliographical references and index.
1. Terrorists—United States.   2. Terrorism—Religious
aspects—Islam.   3. Muslims—United States.   4. Islamic
fundamentalism.   I. Title.
HV6432.H477 2011
363.3250973—dc22   2010053585

ISBN 978-0-307-88525-8
eISBN 978-0-307-88527-2

PRINTED IN THE UNITED STATES OF AMERICA

Jacket design by David Tran
Jacket photograph by Just One Film/Getty Images

10 9 8 7 6 5 4 3 2 1

First Edition

For my parents and for those who serve

CONTENTS

THE NEXT WAVE

PROLOGUE

Guantánamo Bay, Cuba

Latitude: 19 degrees 54 minutes north

Longitude: 75 degrees 9 minutes west

June 5, 2008

0900 hours

The courthouse is imposing: a large metal box. Several rings of fencing surround it. The barbs on the wire are three inches long and razor sharp. They glint in the sunlight. It is custom built for the trial of the century: that of the five 9/11 suspects. Almost two dozen lawyers, both civilian and military, and a handful of translators are present.

Just before 0900, the temperature is nearly eighty degrees, and it feels much hotter. There are two screening checkpoints. IDs are shown. No bags, no electronics, no water bottles with labels are allowed in court. After some prodding, a young man with the Coast Guard explains that the detainees think they are being poisoned if their water bottles look different from ours.

There is no name patch on his uniform. Many of the sailors don't want to be identified. They don't want their families harassed. They didn't ask for the Guantánamo assignment in the first place. When their fellow soldiers come back from Afghanistan and Iraq, they get a pat on the back, a well-done and a thank-you. Those who return from Guantánamo speak of sneers and dirty looks.

With surveillance cameras trained down on us, the ACLU observers and others are having a smoke. We are waiting in the gravel courtyard for the final okay to enter. When the courthouse door opens, a blast of cold air hits us. Crossing the threshold, I wonder if Khalid Sheikh Mohammed, the self-described architect of 9/11, and his four co-conspirators ever feel Cuba's oppressive heat or scan the picture-perfect waves of the Atlantic. Guantánamo Bay is a place where absurd thoughts intrude with regularity.

Every journalist signs in. We are shown to our seats. Reinforced glass separates us from the accused terrorists. They are no more than fifteen yards away. I am in the front row, just to the left of a pillar, with a fairly good vantage point. From what I can see, most of the men are not shackled. They wear white slip-on sneakers with no laces, like little girls.

I have covered most of the big terrorism trials, and experience has taught me that the most important moments come when court is not in session. This pretrial period lives up to my expectations.

At the front left side of the court is the man himself—Khalid Sheikh Mohammed. There is no resemblance to his mug shot that we, covering the trial, refer to as the terrorist's John Belushi period. The disheveled hair and white T-shirt have been replaced by a head covering and a long white robe. His beard is now gray and well over six inches long. His glasses are military issue with thick black frames.

Khalid Sheikh Mohammed is smiling. Though the sound, which is controlled by the military, is turned off or is at least very low, we can see KSM gesturing wildly with his hands and talking at the top of his lungs. He greets his fellow co-conspirators like old friends at a high school reunion.

The men are survivors. They withstood the worst the U.S. government could throw at them. The waterboarding, sleep deprivation, and pressure positions at the CIA secret prisons did not destroy them.

I am distracted by the sound of scratching. The sketch artist, Janet Hamlin, who watched 9/11 unfold from a rooftop in Brooklyn, is feverishly drawing on her sketch pad. First, she lays out the raw outline of the courtroom and the men. Color comes next. I jerk myself back because an extraordinary scene is unfolding before me. Khalid Sheikh Mohammed is now motioning to the others. He wants them to follow his lead. He waves a single defiant finger in the air when he senses dissent from his plan.

Khalid Sheikh Mohammed is already working the system. He wants the 9/11 conspirators to act as their own attorneys. He mocks the proceeding by calling it "an inquisition." His delivery and body language suggest he's been practicing the line in his cell.

KSM understands us better than we understand him. He knows that whatever he says will be reported around the world.

A military source says KSM devours every story, every Web posting, every TV clip about him. Without question, he is al Qaeda's media whore.

And then things get really crazy. For some unknown reason, a court security officer who is making decisions way above his pay grade thinks it's a good idea for KSM to review Janet's sketch. It's the one where he dominates the picture.

Turns out, KSM hates the sketch. He says the nose is all wrong. It's too big or too ethnic or too something. It has to be fixed. KSM orders the sailors to get Janet his FBI mug shot. Apparently, he prefers this picture because he looks composed. His clothes are pressed.

So Janet fixes the sketch to Khalid Sheikh Mohammed's satisfaction. Within minutes, the sketch is carried to our live shot position on the tarmac about fifty yards from the courthouse. It is filmed by the pool TV crew and then broadcast to millions.

Later in the evening, I sit on the equipment box near the live shot position. The sun is dropping like a red hot ball into the Cuban hills.

"Who's in control?" I say under my breath. "Us or the terrorists?"

· · ·

The five 9/11 suspects are al Qaeda's old guard. It would crush their mammoth egos to know that they would soon be yesterday's news because the next wave of recruits was about to crash on America's shores.

There is Faisal Shahzad. On a Saturday night in May 2010, the naturalized American of Pakistani descent drove a crude car bomb into Times Square. Though Shahzad was trained by the Pakistani Taliban, his bomb failed to explode. Unrepentant to the end, the thirty-one-year-old was sentenced to life in prison.

There is Najibullah Zazi. Just three months earlier, the Denver airport shuttle bus driver, who was born in Afghanistan and raised in Pakistan and the United States, pleaded guilty to an al Qaeda plot to blow up the New York City subway system. He was trained overseas by Osama bin Laden's network.

And there is Major Nidal Hasan. The Army psychiatrist allegedly shot to death thirteen at Fort Hood in Texas, including twelve soldiers, one of them pregnant. Shortly after 1330 on November 5, 2009, Hasan walked into the Readiness Center, where soldiers get medical checks before and after deployments. According to eyewitness accounts, Hasan opened fire as he shouted, "Allahu Akbar," which means "God is great." It took the Obama administration nine weeks to publicly acknowledge the Fort Hood massacre as an act of terrorism.

There are cases, like that of Anthony Joseph Tracy, a thirty-five-year-old Virginia man, that do not make national headlines. Described by his court-appointed attorney as a father and a husband, Tracy was arrested for allegedly smuggling 272 Somalis into the United States. Some may have terrorist ties to an al Qaeda affiliate known as al-Shabaab that is based in East Africa. Tracy was held without bond because federal prosecutors said he was a public threat and a flight risk. He was later convicted on human-trafficking charges and sentenced to three years' probation and time served.

The list continues: Omar Hammami in Alabama, Daniel Boyd in North Carolina, Carlos Bledsoe in Arkansas, David Headley and Michael Finton in Illinois, Hosam Smadi in Texas, Betim Kaziu in New York, Tarek Mehanna in Massachusetts.

Analysts may disagree over whether these men truly qualify as al Qaeda members or simply al Qaeda wannabes inspired by the network's message. Although some may be innocent, the number and origin of those charged suggest a pattern.

After 9/11, al Qaeda's top-down structure, much like a Fortune 500 company, splintered and morphed. With the U.S. invasion of Afghanistan, al Qaeda reconstituted in the tribal areas of Pakistan. Recruits still traveled to the camps to get hands-on experience in bomb making and explosives. But by 2006, there had been a perceptible shift.

As CIA director Leon Panetta warned Congress in February 2010, al Qaeda's tactics were evolving. The new recruits were in their twenties, with clean backgrounds. They were hard to detect. Many no longer made the obligatory pilgrimage to Pakistan and Afghanistan for training. Instead, they traveled to Yemen or Somalia. Some were radicalized right here in America.

In a growing number of cases, al Qaeda's followers are just like us. They are educated here, sometimes born here. The radicalization process is compressed. An offbeat loner can reach out and become a dedicated killer in a matter of months.

In the late 1990s, when I was a foreign correspondent based in London, I talked, over warm beers in a pub, with a former weapons inspector in Iraq. He gave me a piece of advice that still rings true today: "Catherine," he said, "terrorism is like water. It takes the path of least resistance. You move one way and it moves another. It is a thinking enemy."

Al Qaeda and its attack on our country continue to shape my life and career. To my knowledge, I am the only network TV correspondent to cover 9/11 in New York, to report on the war on terror from Washington, D.C., for nearly a decade, and to follow the narrative of Khalid Sheikh Mohammed and his four co-conspirators to a military court at Guantánamo Bay.

I live in a military family, so my perspective is different from most correspondents'. I am not sitting on the sidelines reporting the story. I am feeling the impact. In 2009, my husband, an Air Force major and West Point graduate, was deployed to Kandahar, Afghanistan, the birthplace of the Taliban. For nine months, I was a single parent with two children under five. Phone calls late at night made me nervous.

When I investigate the future of al Qaeda, it's personal. I need to know what my family and our nation are in for. What I see, through my reporting, is a growing body of evidence that al Qaeda's American recruits are already here.

CHAPTER 1

MADE IN THE USA

Fox News Channel, Washington, D.C.
November 5, 2009
1700 hours

The overhead paging system is sounding. It cuts through the newsroom like a knife: "Catherine Herridge to Studio 3 . . . Catherine Herridge to Studio 3." I am up, out of my office, and walking quickly through the corridor, past the wall-mounted TVs that monitor CNN, MSNBC, ABC, and Fox Business.

The banners across the lower third of the screens all read "Breaking News" or "Shooting at Soldier Readiness Center Fort Hood."

Just a few minutes earlier, the phone call came in from our producer, who's working his contacts over at the Justice Department. "I got the shooter's name," he says softly and deliberately.

The Justice Department press room is small—about twenty-five by thirty feet. About a dozen reporters for radio, TV, and the wire services are packed in. Close quarters dictate kindness and good manners. But when news breaks, the competitive instinct kicks in. "It sounds Arabic. He may be Muslim," the producer whispers. He doesn't want to tip off the competition.

Four hours into the shooting, a scenario is starting to gel. It appears that there was an attack carried out by a lone gunman, but there may be a second shooter still on the loose. A simultaneous attack is one of the hallmarks of terrorism.

The Muslim name is like a bomb waiting to be triggered. As I hang up the phone, we know senior editorial executives in New York, otherwise known as the "second floor," will vet the name before it makes air. At cable and the big three networks, it's standard practice to run sensitive information up the flagpole before broadcast.

"Do you have a prompter?" the studio tech Mary Pat asks as I sit down.

I can't respond. My brain is locked on the name Nidal Hasan. I repeat it under my breath. Nidal Hasan. Hasan? Is it Pakistani or Palestinian?

The camera is eight feet away. Studio 3 is cool. All of the studios are at least ten degrees below normal room temperature so the equipment won't overheat.

There is no script in the prompter. There is no time to write. I look down at my notes. They will be my only guide.

The voice in my ear is the New York audio tech checking me

in. "Miss Herridge, this is New York audio. Can you hear the programming?"

I adjust my earpiece, then the volume control on my right side. I can hear anchor Shepard Smith carrying the air.

Right now, as the information flows in, we are drilling down on who is responsible for the shooting. I can't go with Hasan's name yet, so I follow the old reporter's rule, "Lead with what you know."

"Law enforcement says everyone involved was military. I asked, do you know they [were] military or were they just wearing military uniforms?" I try to pause before continuing. "Because there's a distinction."

"There certainly is," Smith interjects. He is smooth and smart. Smith is a reporter's anchor because he's been in the trenches himself. Right now, the details are extremely fluid. Eyewitness accounts are notoriously unreliable. Breaking news is like walking a tightrope without a net.

None of us know where the story is going. But increasingly, my gut tells me it will be more than a soldier with a case of post-traumatic stress disorder. It would be too convenient and too easy for the Army to sweep the shooting under the rug.

"Based on the conversations I have had, FBI is engaged, Homeland Security is engaged, and those within the intelligence community who measure the threats inside the U.S. every day."

As I ad-lib for the camera, my mind is skipping from one detail to the next. I need to get the prospect of terrorism on the map without getting the PC police on my back.

"I just want to lay out for you some of the markers that [the investigators] will be considering in the coming hours as to whether this was the act of a lone gunman in the military or whether this may be something even more sinister than that."

Smith holds his questions.

"They will look at the number of shooters. They will look at whether there was a level of coordination and a level of pre-meditation. Was there meant to be a series of shootings that would be simultaneous? Because that is one of the hallmarks of a terrorist attack . . . Was there a conspiracy? . . . Was it a lone-wolf scenario or an ideology?"

"Catherine is not speculating on this matter," Smith explains during the broadcast. "She is telling us what the authorities will be going through as they try to determine the bigger picture of what is happening here."

The segment is wrapping. Twenty-four-hour news is on to the next reporter, the next analyst, the next nugget of information. Thirteen are now dead at Fort Hood. Around thirty others are injured. All were gunned down in ten minutes. It is the worst mass shooting on a military base in U.S. history.

· · ·

On the morning of November 5, 2009, the weather in Washington, D.C., was cool and crisp. Fall was here and the early-morning frost was blanketing the Mall. As I loaded our two kids, five-year-old Jamie and three-year-old Peter, into the old red Volkswagen for school, Army psychiatrist Major Nidal Malik Hasan was making the final preparations for his massacre at Fort Hood.

One day earlier, Hasan's neighbors reported, he began giving away most of his possessions, including food, appliances, and furniture. He claimed he was being deployed. By the early-morning hours of November 5, Hasan, who had just turned thirty-nine, was apparently saying his good-byes. A couple who lived nearby reported that Hasan thanked them for their friendship in a voice mail. He then left to attend dawn prayers.

Not long after, Hasan was picked up on surveillance video at a 7-Eleven carrying a drink and wearing traditional Arab clothing. In the video obtained by CNN, he seemed relaxed as he looked over the counters at the candy and appeared to exchange small talk with the clerk.

Little suggested that in a matter of hours Hasan would, according to eyewitnesses, quietly enter the Readiness Center at Fort Hood and open fire.

Major Hasan's journey began in Arlington, Virginia, in 1970. His parents came from the Middle East, presumably to find a better life for their children. He went to college and eventually joined the Army, where he became a psychiatrist. He didn't wake up one morning with extremist views. It was like a cancer that grew inside him.

By December 17, 2008, nearly a year before the shooting, a strange e-mail relationship caught the attention of the Joint Terrorism Task Forces in San Diego and Washington, D.C. The JTTFs are specialized teams of investigators and analysts from a dozen intelligence and law enforcement agencies. In this case, intelligence agencies intercepted e-mail traffic between the Army major and an American-born cleric.

At the time, Anwar al-Awlaki was not a household name, but he was notorious in counterterrorism circles. He was born in Las Cruces, New Mexico, on April 21, 1971. His father, Nasser al-Awlaki, was a foreign student at New Mexico State University along with his wife. As his father pursued higher education in the American system, young Anwar moved with him. First the family traveled to Nebraska, where his father earned a Ph.D. The next stop was the University of Minnesota, where his father worked as a researcher and a faculty member. Precise dates are hard to come by, but sometime in 1977 or 1978 Anwar al-Awlaki left the United States with his family and returned to Yemen.

Twelve years later, when he was nineteen, after attending what was reported to be a secular school in the Yemeni capital city of Sana'a, al-Awlaki returned to his roots in the United States. In 1991 he enrolled in college as a foreign student with a $20,000 scholarship from the U.S. State Department. It was the beginning of his life of fraud. As an American, al-Awlaki was not eligible for the scholarship program, which was funded by the U.S. Agency for International Development.

Colorado State University and its campus at Fort Collins don't seem like a logical choice for a man who would one day become one of the U.S. government's most wanted terrorists. But it made complete sense to al-Awlaki. The engineering school had an excellent reputation. His degree could easily be exploited for ill by a would-be terrorist. It could be handy for building explosives and other weapons. Khalid Sheikh Mohammed took a similar route. He too graduated from an American university, with a degree in mechanical engineering.

After college, al-Awlaki's life took another mysterious turn that would one day haunt investigators. Born in New Mexico, raised in Yemen, and educated in Fort Collins, Colorado, a city of less than 100,000, Awlaki would make San Diego's ghetto his next stop.

In 1996, al-Awlaki became the imam of the al-Rabat Mosque. In the nineties, the neighborhood that stretched along

El Cajon Boulevard was dotted with check-cashing shops and was a haven for gangbangers and hookers.

While neighbors complained about parking problems during Friday prayers and trash cans in their driveways, the mosque provided the perfect cover for al-Awlaki. It was like hiding in plain sight. In a small anteroom at al-Rabat, he met regularly with two of the 9/11 hijackers: Nawaf al-Hazmi and Khalid al-Mihdhar. They were Saudis and dedicated terrorists by the time they arrived in the United States. While they spoke virtually no English, their al Qaeda handlers sent them to Southern California and the ghetto of San Diego to find a temporary home. The twenty-nine-year-old al-Awlaki was already there, eager and ready to help.

By January 2001, as the 9/11 plot entered its final stages, al-Awlaki had moved from San Diego to Falls Church, Virginia, where he became the imam of the Dar al-Hijra Islamic Center. It was a huge step up from the ghetto. The San Diego mosque was home to about two hundred or three hundred followers. Falls Church offered the charismatic young preacher the opportunity to reach as many as a thousand faithful, and possibly more during Friday prayers.

In Falls Church, al-Awlaki crossed paths with another one of Bin Laden's golden boys, the pilot Hani Hanjour. Now three of the nineteen hijackers, all Saudis, were apparently under the American cleric's wing. Hanjour, al-Hazmi, and al-Mihdhar had another thing in common: they were three of the five hijackers who took over American Airlines Flight 77. Traveling at 530 miles per hour, it slammed into the Pentagon. Fifty-three passengers, six crew members, and 125 people on the ground were killed instantly along with the hijackers.

The FBI was so concerned that, in the first eight days after the attacks, al-Awlaki was interviewed at least four times by the Bureau about his contacts with the hijackers. But as we will discover, new evidence suggests that the American cleric was an overlooked key player in the 9/11 plot itself.

However, in those anxious days after 9/11, al-Awlaki was quite the imam about town. Because of his citizenship, his smooth manner, and his studious-looking glasses, al-Awlaki was a natural with the media. A go-to guy after the attacks for sound bites in near-perfect American English, he popped up on local TV and national broadcasts, including on PBS.

Al-Awlaki was a striking figure. As PBS journalist Ray Suarez noted after a lengthy interview, al-Awlaki knew how to "dance right up to the edge of condoning violence, taking the side of anti-American forces in the Muslim world, and then, just as carefully, reel it back in . . . covering the sharp-edge scalpel of his words in a reassuring sheath."

The *Washington Post* even shot a video profile of al-Awlaki for its Web site. Called "Understanding Ramadan: A Day in the Life of an Imam," it was like a big wet kiss for the cleric. The opening scene showed al-Awlaki eating his morning meal before sunrise and explaining the virtue of fasting before he left for dawn prayers. Later, the reporter hopped into al-Awlaki's gray minivan for a tour of suburban Virginia. As they passed convenience stores and gas stations, al-Awlaki suddenly sharpened his rhetoric: "I think, in general, Islam is presented in a negative way. I mean there is always this association between Islam and terrorism when that is not true at all. Islam is a religion of peace," al-Awlaki said forcefully.

As he walked up the path to his modest red brick house, the cleric's narration of the video continued. "For me personally, I don't see any difference between war [during] Ramadan or in another time of year. Either the war is justified or not. In my personal opinion, I feel that the U.S. rushed into this war. There could have been some other avenues to solve this problem."

Six months earlier, in the spring of 2001, al-Awlaki had presided over the funeral of Major Nidal Hasan's mother at the Falls Church mosque. There, in suburban Virginia, their two lives intersected.

. . .

Washington, D.C.
November 9, 2009
Four days after Fort Hood Massacre
06:12:35

My BlackBerry pings. As I reach for it on the nightstand, I know that at this time of the morning, it could be very important.

My eyes are adjusting to the neon glow of the screen. Sent: 06:12:35 From: DKDraper.

I've known David Draper for six years. He has never impressed me as an early-morning type. He's with a group of earnest investigators who, after 9/11, have made it their business to track the terrorist threat. Their group, the NEFA Foundation, is one of the leading Web sites for jihadist literature, radical Web postings, al Qaeda magazines, and expert analysis.

Draper and his fellow investigators are often ahead of the curve. It takes years to break into their club. A phone call from a principal analyst at NEFA is a sign you've finally passed the sniff test.

On the phone, David's voice is deep and measured. "Early this morning, Evan [Kohlmann, a NEFA investigator] found a statement from Anwar al-Awlaki. Awlaki says Hasan is a hero."

The e-mail chain with Fox's Washington bureau begins. I am still in my pajamas. First I contact the editorial manager, then the bureau chief. I tell them that the Web statement is real. None of these guys, Osama bin Laden's deputies, make false statements or fake tapes. They don't impersonate one another. It's the one area where there is honor among terrorists.

I race to work, my short dark hair still wet and the zipper on my dress halfway done up. There, I open the file, simply titled "Major Nidal Hassan [*sic*] Did the Right Thing." In it, the American-born cleric is effusive in his praise.

As I read, al-Awlaki's power is clear. He is relatively young, just thirty-eight at the time. His command of English is impressive. As one counterterrorism official put it, al-Awlaki is relevant. He gets us. He gets our politics. He strikes at our weakest point.

As I scroll through the e-mail, Major Nidal Hasan is in the ICU at Brooke Army Medical Center in San Antonio, Texas. Early reports indicate he is paralyzed from the waist down. He is on a ventilator. His lawyer, John Galligan, later tells me that Hasan was struck multiple times. He won't say how many bullets Hasan took, nor will Galligan say where he was hit in the spine.

Awlaki writes, "[Hasan] is a man of conscience who could not bear living the contradiction of being a Muslim and serving in an army that is fighting against his own people. . . . The U.S. is leading the war against terrorism which in reality is a war against Islam."

Not long after al-Awlaki's praise of Hasan, the cleric's Web site is pulled down. It looks like the handiwork of the U.S. government, but no one will publicly take the credit.

As I lean back from my desk, a picture is emerging. Al-Awlaki is a clear and present danger. He inspires those who commit violence. In some cases, he blesses their missions. In almost every case, he never meets the jihadist in person. Al-Awlaki is a virtual recruiter.

At 0818, another e-mail drops into my in-box. It's from Evan Kohlmann, the investigator who found Awlaki's statement. Evan is already three steps ahead on the story. He wants to know if Major Hasan is reading a work by al-Awlaki called "Constants on the Path of Jihad." "When the Ft. Dix plotters were driving round and planning their rampage, they were listening to Awlaki's 'Constants' on the car stereo," Evan explains.

. . .

Fort Dix is a large Army installation in southern New Jersey. In 2007, a group of young Muslim men, mostly ethnic Albanians, were arrested and charged with plotting to attack the base. In March of that year, undercover surveillance showed some of the men espousing the virtues of al-Awlaki's lectures. Eljvir Duka, one of the plotters, was so revved up about al-Awlaki's "Constants on the Path of Jihad" that he exhorted an unidentified friend to download a copy. "He gives it to you raw and uncut," Eljvir insisted. "This is the truth. I don't give a damn what everybody says, this is Islam, this is the truth right here. So he doesn't sugar coat. He doesn't have any boundaries to the truth in this."

Beyond the al-Awlaki connection, the Fort Dix plot was bizarre. The men did their reconnaissance while delivering pizzas.

In the spring of 2009, four of the men were given life sentences for conspiring to commit murder against military personnel, while a fifth was sentenced to thirty-three years. A sixth member of the group was deemed a minor player. He was sentenced to twenty months on weapons charges.

Al-Awlaki's influence can also be found north of the border. The Toronto 18 were accused of conspiring to strike major targets, including the Canadian Security Intelligence Service, also known as CSIS; the CBC, a national television network; and the Parliament buildings. The plot was never executed, but some in the group drew their inspiration from al-Awlaki by watching his videos at a makeshift training camp.

One of Osama bin Laden's stated goals was the creation of an ideology that could go global. Instead of a Big Mac or a Coke, Bin Laden served up his brand of religious intolerance. Al-Awlaki was one of al Qaeda's rising stars. Through his blog, his online lectures, e-mail, and social networking sites, including Facebook, he was reaching thousands.

By December 2007, al-Awlaki was hiding in Yemen. According to the head of the National Counterterrorism Center (NCTC), which analyzes real-time threats to the United States, Yemen was an emerging hub for al Qaeda just two years later.

Al Qaeda in Yemen, also known as al Qaeda in the Arabian Peninsula, burst onto the scene in February 2009, when two former Guantánamo detainees announced they were part of the senior leadership. In a roughly produced video obtained by NEFA, former prisoner number 372, Said al-Shehri, thanked his supporters for sticking by him during the long years at the military prison. Former prisoner number 333, Mohammed al-Awfi, said payback was coming for Christian nations at war against Muslims.

Eighteen months after the Obama administration promised to close the military prison at Guantánamo Bay, roughly half of the remaining detainees were from Yemen. The U.S. military couldn't send them home. The American people didn't want them here. And no third country would take them. So the Yemeni detainees made the best of it. They spent their days on crude StairMasters in open-air cells, eating a nutritious diet of up to 6,000 calories a day. For some detainees obesity had become a major problem.

Yemen is a country the size of California and Pennsylvania combined, resting on the Gulf of Aden, across from the Horn of Africa. The dominant religion is Islam, but there are small pockets of Jews and Christians. The country was extraordinarily unstable. The government was in a bind. It was juggling a strong secessionist movement in the south, a rebel insurgency in the north, and dwindling natural resources. Al Qaeda seemed the least of the Yemeni government's problems.

The Clinton, Bush, and Obama administrations should have known better. With explosives packed in an open scow masquerading as a garbage boat, al Qaeda ripped a gaping hole in the USS *Cole* in the Yemeni port of Aden in October 2000. At the time, the attack that killed seventeen American sailors was seen as another example of al Qaeda getting lucky. In fact, it was the seminal attack before 9/11.

Al Qaeda was proving itself to be an astute enemy—one that always learned from its mistakes. A virtually identical operation had been mounted against the USS *The Sullivans* ten months earlier, in January 2000. The terrorists were so ambitious and the explosives were so heavy that the suicide vessel sank. On the second go-round, the explosives salvaged by al Qaeda were loaded into the now-strengthened boat.

The commander of the USS *Cole,* Kirk Lippold, told me that the blast site was forty feet by forty feet, the size of a two-story house. Jagged edges of steel lined the rim like the teeth of a great white shark. It was a well-conceived and clever plot, Lippold explained. Rather than ram the ship, the terrorists pulled their scow up alongside the *Cole*'s hull. At 1118, the chow line was open early so the crew could set sail by afternoon. Engine room number 1 and the galley took the full force of the explosion. Many of the *Cole* families tell the same story. They buried their sons and daughters two, even three times. The Navy kept finding more of their remains.

For an ambitious and industrious young man like al-Awlaki, eight years after the *Cole* attack Yemen was an ideal place to operate. His father, a former government minister, was respected and well connected. Al-Awlaki's tribe was also behind him. Always thinking one step ahead, al-Awlaki used his base to build bridges to other like-minded groups. Simply put: al-Awlaki was expanding his brand.

In February 2008, the State Department added a little-known group to its roster of terrorist organizations. Based in Somalia and known as al-Shabaab or the Mujahideen Youth Movement, the network was busy recruiting young Americans. For the most part, the recruits were U.S. citizens of Somali descent who were tapped to wage jihad in their parents' homeland. Former CIA director Michael Hayden told me that the Ethiopian push into Somalia to stop the spread of radical Islam catalyzed the expat Somali population. In the United States, young men connected with al-Shabaab online or with the help of a local recruiter.

As 2008 came to a close, al-Awlaki sent a salutation to his al-Shabaab brothers in East Africa. The American's communiqué was glowing in its praise. "We are following your recent news and it fills our hearts with immense joy," al-Awlaki wrote with enthusiasm. He said the network was successfully expanding the reach of Sharia, or strict Islamic law. Like a loyal political operative, al-Awlaki encouraged readers to open their wallets. "Their [al-Shabaab's] success depends on your support. It is the responsibility of the ummah [the Islamic community] to help them with men and money."

Winding up his sales pitch, al-Awlaki said that he would join the fight but that other responsibilities prevented his doing so. "Dear brothers may Allah guide you and grant you victory. Only Allah knows that if my circumstances would have allowed I would not have hesitated in joining you and being a soldier in your ranks."

Whether he knew it or not, al-Awlaki was identifying a growth market. Since late 2007, nearly two dozen men from Minneapolis, all Americans of Somali descent, had disappeared into al-Shabaab's training camps. Though the group's goal was to train Americans to fight the remnants of Somalia's secular government, the fear remained that these U.S. citizens would return one day and use their battlefield skills at home.

The Western mouthpiece for al-Shabaab was an American from Daphne, Alabama. Fox News Channel was the first to identify Omar Hammami as an al Qaeda propagandist. The feds now consider him an active threat. If Hammami ever ventures back to Alabama, there is a federal indictment waiting for him. It accuses Hammami of providing material support to a terrorist organization. It is a boilerplate charge that carries about fifteen years in prison. The mainstream media ignored our reporting until the *New York Times Magazine* made Hammami its cover story in the spring of 2010, five months after Fox first identified him.

In September 2009, Daphne was hot like a frying pan. A town of about twenty thousand, it was a stone's throw from Mobile. With street signs like "Whispering Pines Road," Daphne was small-town America.

We needed to break the story right away. Our Justice Department producer, Mike Levine, had arrived two days earlier. We believed that CBS's *60 Minutes* was chasing the Hammami story too. One of their crews was apparently sighted in Daphne a few days before we arrived, but they didn't come up with the goods.

We set up the satellite truck for live reporting at the gas station across from Hammami's old high school. Daphne High was a place full of southern hospitality and tradition. Sports ruled. Students and teachers were friendly. Even the attendant at the gas station's minimart was brimming with news tips about Hammami's old pals.

Fox's arrival was big news in Daphne, and Hammami's old acquaintances were doing drive-bys with their high school yearbooks. "I think you can find his old girlfriend working at the Olive Garden," one woman offered. Another woman said Hammami seemed freaked-out around girls after his conversion to Islam.

How a young American left Daphne behind for a journey that took him to Canada and Egypt before he became the Western face of al Qaeda's Somali affiliate cannot be fully explained. The FBI doesn't need more evidence to know that recruits like Hammami, with American passports, can be hard to stop at the border.

FBI director Robert Mueller testified before the Senate

Committee on Homeland Security and Governmental Affairs in September 2009 that the threat from American recruits, like Hammami, was real and growing. The first documented case of an American suicide bomber was Minneapolis native Shirwa Ahmed, who, like Hammami, was a member of al-Shabaab. Ahmed blew himself up in northern Somalia in 2008.

Ahmed was described by his hometown newspaper, the *Minneapolis Star Tribune,* as a "shy young man who liked basketball, hip-hop, and girls." His remains were pulled from a bomb crater in the port town of Bosasso. There were simultaneous car bombings across the breakaway region of Somaliland. The Ethiopian embassy was hit. Two car bombs hit the Puntland intelligence headquarters. Within hours of the attack, FBI investigators were called in. To their astonishment, an American was found.

Federal law enforcement sources believed the twenty-six-year-old university student was radicalized in Minneapolis. Ahmed was buried near his hometown in a traditional Muslim ceremony after he was identified through DNA. The FBI investigation into al-Shabaab eventually stretched from Minneapolis to Seattle, San Diego, Columbus, Boston, Atlanta, Alexandria, Virginia, and Daphne, Alabama.

At their core, al Qaeda and like-minded extremists seek to exploit our social sensitivities. American women were a logical next step. In the spring of 2010, the Department of Justice unsealed indictments against two female suspects. Both were lonely. Both were looking for love. The search did not take them to a dating Web site. It led them to a trap apparently laid by al Qaeda sympathizers.

Colleen LaRose lived in suburban Philadelphia. She was in

her midforties. Based on her Facebook page and an old mug shot, she looked like a bar girl who was well past her prime. One investigator later told me that anyone who used the handle "JihadJane" on the Web probably wanted to get caught.

Despite her lack of sophistication, the charges against LaRose were serious. She was accused of conspiring to provide material support to a terrorist organization. She was also accused of conspiring to kill in a foreign country. The Swedish artist Lars Vilks was in her crosshairs. LaRose and her co-conspirators wanted the lanky, then sixty-three-year-old Swede dead. He'd made the mistake of drawing the prophet Muhammad with the body of a dog.

LaRose was a blond, blue-eyed American with a clean passport who could travel with ease. She was allegedly an ideal and willing recruit for an overseas operation. She was ordered by an unindicted co-conspirator to kill the Swedish artist in a way that would frighten "the whole Kufar [non-believer] world." Prosecutors also alleged she was willing to steal for the cause. A passport ripped off from an old boyfriend was supposed to grease the skids for one of the "brothers." In August 2009, LaRose left relative obscurity in suburban Philadelphia for Europe "with the intent to live and train with jihadists." LaRose eventually pled guilty to the charges. She admitted using the Internet to make contact with foreign jihadists.

In April 2010, Jamie Paulin-Ramirez flashed across the cable networks as "Jihad Jamie." She was also tall and blond and lost. In a Philadelphia federal court for her arraignment, Paulin-Ramirez shuffled to the defense desk with a blank look in her eyes—so blank that I asked her defense attorney after court whether she was slow or mildly retarded. He didn't answer the question directly, but he hinted that the government might have a hard time proving his client fully understood the implications of her actions.

During the arraignment, she huddled with her lawyer. Paulin-Ramirez was twelve weeks pregnant. The father was believed to be an Algerian man, an unindicted co-conspirator in the case. Prosecutors alleged that the day she arrived in Europe to join the training camp, she married a man whom she had never before met in person. Her life seemed to be one train wreck after another.

At least four government lawyers, including a heavyweight from the Justice Department, were on hand for the brief court appearance. For good measure, federal agents lined the back wall of the room. They stood with their legs slightly spread and their hands behind their backs.

Paulin-Ramirez and her lawyer asked the judge for a concession. While there were no cameras, there was an audiotape of the hearing. Because her lawyer believed there were phone calls, voice mails, and other surveillance against his client, he didn't want her voice entered into the record. When asked to enter a plea, Jihad Jamie shook her head from side to side. It was a no for not guilty.

As I rode down in the elevator, the scene played out in my mind. It looked like the old government sledgehammer was at work to take out a basket case. Even Jihad Jamie's mother, Christine Mott, who did the obligatory rounds on the national breakfast TV shows, implied that her daughter was not playing with a full deck. She told Fox that Jihad Jamie was lonely and insecure, and had no idea what she was getting into.

Before Paulin-Ramirez left Leadville, Colorado, a town of 2,700, her mother said, her views shifted. She hitched her wagon to radical Islam, moved to Ireland, and joined a group that allegedly wanted to kill the same Swedish cartoonist. Mott said that her grandson, nicknamed "Baby Huey," went with his mother. Pretty soon, he was calling Granny telling her that "Christians needed to be punished."

In March 2011, Paulin-Ramirez admitted to helping a terrorist cell. She faced up to fifteen years in prison. Her lawyer told the Reuters news service that Paulin-Ramirez had also lost her pregnancy.

Washington, D.C.
Near Fort McNair
December 14, 2009
2300

"What do you want for Christmas?" I ask my husband.

It's late and both kids are finally asleep. J.D. is standing near the refrigerator. A tall man with blue eyes that look bleached by the sun and the desert, he is a major with the Air Force. His glory days were special operations with the Army based in Germany. Somalia, Rwanda, the Balkans, and Afghanistan were all in the zone. Now he likes to joke that he is too old and too fat to do crazy things like kill the bad guys.

"I don't want to visit relatives," J.D. says. No explanation is needed. In August he got back from eight months in Afghanistan, and he still needs to decompress. He divided his time between Kandahar, the Taliban hub, and a forward operating base so close to the Pakistani border that, he said, you could throw a quarter over the perimeter fence and it would land in Pakistan. "Okay. If we are not seeing relatives, we'd better have a plan. It will soften the blow." I am dreading the next phone call to both sets of parents.

Thankfully, both families understand. J.D. and I agree on New York City. Five-year-old Jamie is up for the idea because he lost his first tooth there, in a Korean barbecue restaurant. Three-year-old Peter is cool with the plan as long as a Kit Kat is waiting at the other end.

Two weeks later, the car is loaded with the usual child detritus of special blankets and once favorite toys. As we break free of the Washington Beltway, I am fighting the urge to check my BlackBerry.

I know I am weak. I know I will look. I subtly put the Black-Berry between my legs and rest it on the front seat.

"Can you just put it away?" J.D. sends the first of many warning shots. Close-quarters combat can be intense in a Honda Element with two children whose combined age is eight.

I am staring straight ahead at I-95 North. I say nothing, only sigh. We aren't even close to Baltimore yet. Then I unzip my knapsack and slip the evil instrument into a pocket. As I sink back into the front seat, I am reminded that the holidays are a hard time of year for any kind of addict.

I am doing okay until Christmas Day. We do all the usual family stuff that leaves you wondering how you spent $500 before lunch. Radio City Music Hall Rockettes: check. The Disney Store: check. My breath is floating up and over Fifth Avenue as I do the mental arithmetic. FAO Schwarz: check. The snow leopard at the Central Park Zoo: check.

By late afternoon and after at least one drink, I can't stop myself any longer. I finally check my BlackBerry. It is like the first hit for a junkie—only two hundred e-mails since my last day of work!

"As a New Year's resolution, I have got to get myself off of these mailing groups," I mutter under my breath. My thumb spins the ball as I scroll down my in-box. Christmas Day, e-mail traffic is low, but one message warrants attention.

12/25/09 1724

From: Kuban

Subject: Statement by Department of Homeland Security

It says Secretary Janet Napolitano is being briefed about an incident on Northwest Flight 253. Additional screening is being thrown on at the airports. The public is being encouraged to "be observant and aware of their surroundings and report any suspicious behavior or activity to law enforcement officials."

At 1822, another e-mail drops into my box. The initial reports of passengers setting off firecrackers are not panning out. In the hotel basement, with the kids watching videos upstairs in our room, I sit on the carpet in the business center to get my brief. I am writing on a hotel envelope.

My congressional source is plugged into the NYPD Counterterrorism Bureau. We've got a name. Abdulmutallab. He is Nigerian. He is in his twenties. The bomb was in his underwear.

I ask the source to repeat it. I want to be clear about the underwear. The device is fairly sophisticated. The detonator is a syringe taped to the suspect's groin.

The longer I take notes, the more trouble I am in. My husband is pissed. So are my kids. The Christmas break was supposed to be our family time together.

I type up what I know and send it to the Washington news desk. It is filed under new and urgent information. Minutes later, my cell phone rings.

"Can you do a phoner?" I am talking to Jodie Curtis, the

assignment editor on the Washington news desk that evening. She is the point person for getting new information on the air.

When you can't get to the studio quickly, a question-and-answer on the phone is a good solution.

From 2100 until late, I call live into the shows while sitting in my pajamas in the hallway of the hotel, with my notebook propped up on my legs. My congressional source is accurate. The suspect, his nationality, and his age all pan out. Within three days it is clear: the Nigerian is also connected to the American-born cleric. Anwar al-Awlaki is really starting to bother me.

. . .

Umar Farouk Abdulmutallab had barely turned twenty-three when he stuffed explosives between his legs. Blowing up Flight 253 from Amsterdam to Detroit on Christmas Day was his goal. It was a deceptive plot because the wealthy Nigerian fit none of the obvious profiles. For one, he wasn't Middle Eastern. He was educated at elite schools in Africa and in London. Two former CIA officers later told me that they believed the boy's arrogance saved a lot of lives that day.

Given his wealth and privilege, the kid thought he knew better. Puncturing the skin of a jet at twenty-five thousand feet with a small explosive device can blow the plane apart. But Umar Farouk waited until Flight 253 was well into its descent over Detroit before he executed the mission. Maybe nerves or second thoughts got the better of him. The more likely explanation is that the kid liked the idea of blowing up the jet and killing dozens of people on the ground. But at five thousand feet a hole in the skin of the plane is just a hole. The plane will probably land. And the bomber will be toast.

A source familiar with the intelligence told me that al-Awlaki was the middleman between the Nigerian and the bomb maker. We later learned of evidence that al-Awlaki had coached the Nigerian on Western security and surveillance.

In Abdulmutallab's case, the warning signs were there long before the kid got on the plane. A telephone intercept about the "Nigerian" was picked up several months earlier. The father, a wealthy onetime Nigerian banker, was so concerned about his son's extremist views that he went to the U.S. embassy in Nigeria. He spoke to the CIA station chief, the Agency's eyes and ears on the ground. The proverbial dots were not connected. Abdulmutallab got on the plane.

Good analysts saw the crotch bomb coming. Al Qaeda in Yemen had tried a similar attack in the summer of 2009. The suicide bomb targeting the Saudi prince Muhammad bin Nayef was big news in the Middle East. Taking out bin Nayef would have been a twofer of the highest order: assassinating a member of the Saudi royal family and the kingdom's homeland security chief in one blow.

There were various accounts, but one of the most scintillating went like this: The bomber, who was a wanted terrorist, turned himself in. As a gesture of goodwill, the Saudis waved the bomber through screening into the palace. As he neared the prince, the bomber stumbled, either because he was nervous or by tripping over a bump in the tiles. The bomber fell, and the impact triggered the explosion. Some reports described explosives packed in a condom. They were apparently hidden in a body cavity. You can work out the rest.

Later identified in a martyrdom video, the bomber was surprisingly young. He had the sparse beard of a teenager. His name was Abdullah Hassan Taleh al-Asiri. He was one of the kingdom's eighty-five most wanted terrorists. We have the FBI's ten most wanted fugitives or terrorists; given the scale of their problem, the Saudis have to think much bigger. The prince was lightly injured, according to Saudi government reports. Pretty soon, the tale of the "butt bomber" took on a life of its own. The British press dubbed him the "body bomber." And the best headline of all—QAEDA 'ASS'ASSIN—belonged to the *New York Post.*

. . .

On September 11, the enemy was sent here to kill us. The nineteen hijackers took advantage of our hospitality, our lack of rules, and our bureaucratic system. In those days, Phoenix FBI agents had warned their superiors of suspicious Arab men flight-training in the heartland. The memos were ignored. The evil intentions of nineteen men were realized.

It is important to learn from the past. But if you spend all your time looking in the rearview mirror, wondering why you didn't connect the dots, you will cause an accident right in front of you.

Now, two new threat pictures are emerging. The first includes American passport holders who travel overseas to the tribal areas of Pakistan, to Yemen, or to Africa for hands-on training. They return to the United States at will. With no criminal record, it is hard to stop them at the border. The second includes Americans radicalized here in the comfort of their own homes. Through chat rooms on the Web, they find like-minded people. Their hate of the United States binds them together.

Now, the enemy can be overseas. It can also be your neighbor.

By the winter of 2009, the next wave of American recruits, including al-Awlaki, had become my reporting obsession, culminating in the TV broadcast *Fox News Reporting: The American Terrorist.* Join me. Clear off the passenger seat in the old red Volkswagen as we travel to Capitol Hill, to the bars and to the street corners where discreet conversations take place. Sit with me. Clear off the desk as we leaf through faded old documents to piece together the past.

What we discover together will surprise and anger you. It will change your view of the future. It will also change how you see those behind the 9/11 attacks.

CHAPTER 2

THE DIGITAL JIHADIST

Washington, D.C.

March 10, 2010

1400 hours

Your file is corrupted."

I hit the Return key again. It just can't be.

"Your file is corrupted."

Iggy, the computer wizard at New York's IT help desk, is on the line. He's a handy guy who could probably hack into a secure government Web site if he set his mind to it.

Iggy is calm. I am nearly hysterical.

"Whoever sent you this Web link really doesn't want you to have this audiotape anymore."

Since the Fort Hood shooting, I've had two goals. I want the e-mails exchanged between the alleged shooter, Army major Nidal Hasan, and the American-born cleric Anwar al-Awlaki. I also want an interview with al-Awlaki, but one of my intelligence contacts says it's a bad idea. A drone might lock on to my satellite phone signal. And bingo, we're both dead. Though my contact is half joking, we both understand that the U.S. government wants the cleric gone.

The story behind the cleric's audiotape begins with a mysterious phone call a week earlier. A Middle Eastern contact knows what I am looking for. He sends me a message late one afternoon. He says it is time to talk. "My friend has an interview with the cleric. Are you interested?" My contact pauses. "However, it will cost you some money."

At Fox we don't pay for interviews, but I can't let this one drop.

"How much does he want?" I ask.

Without missing a beat, my contact lays out the demands. "He wants $30,000."

I nearly choke. My contact keeps talking. "It will get you exclusive rights. Soon, you will receive a sample of the tape. You can decide then. Yes or no."

A few hours later, an e-mail drops into my box. I recognize the address. You don't send in the nuns to get the al Qaeda tape.

The audio clip is thirty-four seconds long. The overseas source is smart. He knows it is not enough to be valuable, but there is enough tape to get it authenticated.

I meet Richard (not his real name) in a parking lot. Our conversation goes something like this:

"What would you say, and we are speaking hypothetically, of course . . ." I'm asking a big favor. I need the tape authenticated. And there are only a handful of government bureaus that can do it. "What would you say if I told you that I just got a new tape, or at least a partial clip, from the American cleric al-Awlaki?" I pause and smile. "Hypothetically speaking, of course."

Richard gives me a broad grin. He is an extremely smart man with a good sense of humor. It is a must for those who work in the intelligence world. "Hypothetically, we would be very interested in your tape and how you came to get it, Catherine." Richard is beaming now. The game is starting to get interesting.

"Richard, what would you say if I told you that the clip is on my BlackBerry in the trunk of my red Volkswagen?"

And before Richard can answer, I unlock the trunk, reach inside, and pull out my BlackBerry. I hit the Search function and the e-mail pops up. I activate the speakerphone.

"Wow, that sounds like our boy." Richard is chuckling. "I don't think we knew al-Awlaki had a new tape."

The cleric's voice is distinctive, and within days two government experts authenticate the tape. In return for the favor, they get a full copy of the cleric's audio message before it hits the Web and reaches al-Awlaki's intended audience.

Getting the entire eleven-minute audiotape takes a series of e-mails. First the overseas contact sends the link to a Web site that is an unlikely home for al Qaeda propaganda. The overseas source writes in broken English:

```
it is pleasuere for your replay soon


well, i'll give you the tabe for poublishing within
24 hoours pls


then w'll agree about mony no problem . . . the very im-
portant now poublishing the tabe of Imam Anwar Aulaqi.
```

after you finishing downloading the tabe call me plasea
by my Mobile, for give you a password

I put my cursor on the link. When I hit Return, a woman with exceptionally large breasts pops up—followed by more pornlike material and spam. I am worried I will get pinged at work for looking at porn. How will I explain to Fox legal—it's all part of my research?

I keep typing. The IT help desk manager is now on the line. He is trying to help. He is equally puzzled. "Catherine, I don't think there is anything here except spam, but I will keep trying." With persistence, he gets the file up and open, but it is encrypted.

Fox IT tries multiple programs. The file won't open. The IT manager says I need to go back to the overseas source. We need the program information to unzip it.

Five days after the initial e-mail demanding $30,000, the overseas source isn't talking money anymore. I suspect he is being pressured by al Qaeda in Yemen or its proxies to get al-Awlaki's message out. I now believe the money was a selfish move. Al Qaeda middlemen need to make a living too.

How am I going to get the program information? I ask myself, leaning back in my chair. The deadline for *Special Report with Bret Baier* at 1800 is looming, but it is just a blur in the background. I am thinking strategy.

There is only one way to deal with the situation, I conclude. Falling back on the dumb-woman-needs-a-man's-help game plan rarely fails.

I suck up my pride, and explain on the phone that I am extremely thick when it comes to computers and technical issues.

I would be so grateful if a supersmart and worldly guy like my new overseas source could walk me through the program.

On the phone, the source's English is better than I was led to believe by his e-mails. I conclude that my new source is a smooth operator. The bad English appears to be a ruse.

The dumb-woman routine works like a charm. He takes the bait.

Within twenty-four hours, I have the program information. I've been led to believe that the tape is within Fox's grasp.

Little do I know that another unexpected roadblock is around the corner.

The IT help desk takes the program information. In short order, Iggy gets it rolling. "Catherine, do you have the password? The program is asking for a password."

I want to shoot myself. First it was porn, then spam, followed by an encrypted Web link, and now a password.

I call Yemen. My source is getting nervous. He will no longer use e-mail. He says he will text me the password. I am starting to wonder whether I am tracking a terrorist or Charlie Sheen.

"Can't you tell me over the phone?" I plead. I don't want to lose any more time. My gut tells me the tape is slipping away.

He declines. He probably figures, and rightly so, that the National Security Agency is listening.

Now I am sitting at my desk. No phone calls. No e-mails. I periodically check my BlackBerry for the text. It is still not there. How long does it take to get a text from Yemen? I've never had one before. One minute? Ten minutes?

I decide to get a Coke to kill some time. As I walk to the bureau kitchen, I wonder if the password will be something obvious, like "al Qaeda" or "Bin Laden" or even "Anwar."

Back at my desk, the password box is up on my screen. I am tempted to try all three.

Finally, after the eternity of almost fifteen minutes, the password hits my BlackBerry. As I suspected, it is obvious and idiotproof. I'll let you guess which one.

I slowly type the password. I don't want any mistakes. I hit Return, and the program begins to open. I reach over to my speaker on the desktop and twist the button to Loud.

"All praises due to Allah and may peace and blessings be upon his messenger Muhammad. . . ." It is the cleric, but his distinct voice sounds a little off. I wonder if it got distorted between Yemen and America.

We later learn from a noted forensic audio analyst that al-Awlaki or one of his aides doctored the tape. Something called reverb or echo was added so that the cleric would sound like he was addressing a crowd of thousands, not hiding in a closet.

Panic shoots through me. What if the file unzips only once? I am not recording. I will lose everything!

I hit Pause, then run out of my office, down the hall, past the digital clock with its glowing red numbers, and into master control. The engineers look surprised to see me. Correspondents don't drop in often.

"I need to get a recording on an al Qaeda tape—*fast*. It's on my desktop." Now the engineers look stunned. It is not a typical request.

Seleena Muhammad gets out of her chair. A tall and attractive woman with a firm touch, she directs me to the "Scan-Do" machine in the broadcast control room. It can record video or audio off the Web for broadcast. We typically use it to pick up political attack ads, not al Qaeda messages.

When I get back to my desk, I hit Play. Nothing happens. The file is a one-zip wonder. I made one of the most fundamental errors: I underestimated the overseas source. He is no one's fool.

Iggy on the IT help desk says he will see what he can do. I am not optimistic. I try the cell phone one last time for the overseas source. It rings and rings and rings. Not even voice mail. With the tape delivered, he has gone to ground.

In midafternoon, my office phone rings. I look at the screen. The number is Iggy's. In a very matter-of-fact way, Iggy says he turned al-Awlaki's audiotape into an MP3 file by confusing the program. I nearly fall out of my chair. I have no idea how you "confuse a program," but Iggy has done it! I thank him. I thank his supervisor. I am so high and so happy I thank everyone in sight.

I settle back into my office chair and hit Play. Eleven minutes of the American cleric is heading my way.

Al-Awlaki does not disappoint. He calls attention to the Obama administration's lack of transparency by bringing together the alleged shooter at Fort Hood, Major Nidal Hasan, and the suspect in the attempted Christmas Day bombing, Umar Farouk Abdulmutallab.

> Until this moment, the Administration is refusing to release the e-mails exchanged between myself and Nidal. And after the operation of our brother Umar Farouk the initial comments coming from the Administration were looking the same—another attempt at covering up the truth. But al Qaeda cut off Obama from deceiving the world again by issuing their statement claiming responsibility for the operation.

Given the bad economy, al-Awlaki predicts President Obama will fail.

Following 9/11, the American people gave George W. Bush unanimous backing to fight against the Mujahideen and gave him the blank check to spend as much as needed to fulfill that objective. The result—he failed. And he failed miserably. So, if America failed to defeat the Mujahideen and gave its president unlimited support, how can it win with Obama, who is on a short leash?

In the lecture, al-Awlaki leaves no stone unturned.

I eventually came to the conclusion that Jihad against America is binding upon myself just as it is binding on every other able Muslim.

Days later, I learn through back channels that I had access to al-Awlaki's tape two days before the U.S. government. It's giving some of my law enforcement contacts heartburn. I apparently have a source investigators are not aware of.

· · ·

Al-Awlaki is a virtual recruiter. He doesn't need a mosque. He doesn't need to meet his followers in person. All he needs is a keyboard, some software, and presto—a digital jihadist is born.

Of course, the process is more complex. To fully understand al-Awlaki's power and the potential of others like him, it made the most sense to start with the expert's expert.

Charlie Allen was a legend in the U.S. intelligence community. He spent forty-seven years at the CIA before a three-year term at Homeland Security, where he led intelligence and analysis for the fledgling department.

He rarely gave interviews, but on a crisp winter day, our crew was setting up in a large glass-faced conference room near Thomas Circle. We had an hour.

Whether the subject has been Iraq, Northern Ireland, or Guantánamo Bay, I've learned over the years that the facts have a power all their own. Once Charlie sat down, he owned the interview.

Charlie's backstory could be a book in itself. At the CIA, he served for four years as the intelligence officer for warning. Allen's job was to predict events that would surprise the U.S. government. His job was to answer the question "How do you know what you don't know?"

Allen was incredibly good at it. With a wry smile, he explained why he wrote both "warning of war and warning of attack" in July 1990. Based on the intelligence, Allen could see the future. Iraqi dictator Saddam Hussein would invade Kuwait. It would not be an incursion. Saddam was planning to stay.

On August 1, 1990, Allen came into work at 0500. He reviewed overnight technical intelligence. He knew Saddam was hell-bent on taking down Kuwait. To Allen's dismay, no one was listening. According to Allen, the warning fell on deaf ears at his beloved agency, the CIA. He went AWOL and headed to the White House and to the State Department, and he made calls to the Pentagon. He said time had run out.

Allen feared that the cost of being right would be the abolishment of his position. Allen said that in January 1991, as cruise missiles headed for Baghdad, he spoke with Judge William Webster, then CIA director, for an hour. According to Allen, Webster said he had no plans to abolish Allen's position; instead, he planned to strengthen it.

I told you Allen's story so you would understand his credentials. When he sounds the warning siren, many in the intelligence community sit up and pay attention. In 2008, Allen warned again that a storm was on the horizon.

Allen was preparing a speech for the National Geospatial-Intelligence conference in Nashville, Tennessee. It was one of the intelligence industry's premier events, where the field's glitterati gathered to network and talk shop. Allen was working for Homeland Security at the time, as the undersecretary for intelligence and analysis and the chief intelligence officer.

He read the draft speech. He wasn't satisfied. Something was missing. Allen asked an aide to add a few lines about the American-born cleric Anwar al-Awlaki.

Allen saw the rising threat. Young people were being seduced into thinking that a violent Islamic ideological approach to life was the right way to go. Allen saw the idea taking hold in the United States and Canada. In particular, Allen was troubled by the extraordinary control that al-Awlaki was exerting over these groups.

Allen felt so strongly about the growing use of the Internet as a tool for spreading an extreme message that he insisted that a section of the National Intelligence Estimate (NIE) in 2007 be devoted to the Web.

Once again, Allen saw the future. He instinctively knew that the Web would be one of the most significant drivers of extreme Islam. Once unleashed, the digital legacy of hate lived forever.

After the shooting at Fort Hood, the attempted bombing on Christmas Day 2009, and the failed attack on Times Square in May 2010, reading the "Key Judgments" from the 2007 NIE was a kick in the gut.

We assess that the spread of radical—especially Salafi [Muslims dedicated to restoring the pure Islam practiced by the first generations of Muslims]—Internet sites, increasingly aggressive anti-U.S. rhetoric and actions, and the growing number of radical, self-generating cells in Western countries indicate that the radical and violent segment of the West's Muslim population is expanding, including in the United States. The arrest and prosecution by U.S. law enforcement of a small number of violent Islamic extremists inside the United States—who are becoming more connected ideologically, virtually, and/or in a physical sense to the global extremist movement—points to the possibility that others may become sufficiently radicalized that they will view the use of violence here as legitimate. We assess that this internal Muslim terrorist threat is not likely to be as severe as it is in Europe, however.

The NIE continued:

We assess that globalization trends and recent technological advances will continue to enable even small numbers of alienated people to find and connect with one another, justify and intensify their anger, and mobilize resources to attack—all without requiring a centralized terrorist organization, training camp, or leader.

In plainspeak, the Internet was facilitating terrorism. And some in the U.S. intelligence community were predicting the problem more than two years before a Nigerian man stuffed explosives in his underwear.

The Net allowed like-minded individuals to hook up with

ease. There was no need to leave their homes or go to the mosques, where they feared the FBI was watching them. Once in a virtual community, they could justify their actions to one another, make a plan, set the wheels into motion.

Allen estimated that between four thousand and six thousand jihadist Web sites were active. As of this writing, he believed that several hundred of them were important. As Allen and other noted counterterrorism experts observed, among al-Awlaki's greatest strengths was his strong command of "American" English. He could combine colloquial expressions with his radical interpretation of Islam. An important barrier was now lifted.

"44 Ways to Support Jihad" was one of al-Awlaki's pivotal works and was widely available on the Web in English. My copy came from the NEFA Foundation. "Way" number 29, titled "WWW Jihad," made me pause and reread it several times. It dovetailed with Allen's analysis.

The internet has become a great medium for spreading the call of Jihad and following the news of the mujahideen. Some ways in which the brothers and sisters could be 'internet mujahideen' is by contributing in one or more of the following ways:

It read like a PowerPoint presentation.

Establishing discussion forums that offer a free, uncensored medium for posting information relating to Jihad.

Establishing email lists to share information with interested brothers and sisters.

Posting or emailing Jihad literature and news.

Setting up websites to cover specific areas of Jihad, such as: mujahideen news, Muslim POWs and Jihad literature.

"44 Ways" was accessible using any major search engine at the time, and it got more than ten thousand hits. According to a federal indictment, al-Awlaki's digital lecture appealed to a Texas man with at least ten aliases.

The Barry Walter Bujol Jr. case was brought in the Southern District of Texas. In the summer of 2010, prosecutors alleged that Bujol, a U.S. citizen and resident of Hempstead, Texas, was trying to provide material support to al Qaeda in Yemen. In Bujol's case, "material support" was alleged to include prepaid calling cards, mobile phone SIM cards, Global Positioning System receivers, and a manual on unmanned aerial vehicles (UAVs) commonly used by the U.S. military in Afghanistan.

The Joint Terrorism Task Force began investigating Bujol in 2008. He and al-Awlaki were exchanging e-mails.

In the course of their online relationship, al-Awlaki allegedly sent Bujol a copy of "44 Ways." After that, the feds got interested. A confidential human source was introduced into the case. The source was meant to test whether Bujol was putting al-Awlaki's words into action.

The feds claimed that Bujol told the informant he wanted to travel overseas to fight "violent jihad" for al Qaeda in Yemen. To make it happen, Bujol was given a fake ID by the FBI plant. It bore Bujol's picture. He used the fake ID to access secure zones of a Houston-area port with the alleged goal of boarding a ship bound for the Middle East. Little did Bujol know that it was all a setup. Shortly after he boarded the vessel, FBI agents arrested him.

Al-Awlaki's "44 Ways," CDs, and lectures were all available online. We bought a boxed set on the Web to prepare for the Fox News documentary on al-Awlaki. We found it—no problem. The cleric's message was ours in less than forty-eight hours.

Al-Awlaki was so prolific that it seemed only a matter of time before his work and that of Omar Hammami, our American in Somalia, would come together in a single case.

By 2008 al-Awlaki was busy expanding his brand like a Western corporation. The American cleric was building bridges to the Somali al Qaeda affiliate known as al-Shabaab. Both Americans, al-Awlaki and Hammami, were very active on the Web through lectures, audiotapes, and videos. They were all for free speech.

Late one Saturday night in the summer of 2010, two New Jersey men in their early twenties, both American citizens, were arrested at John F. Kennedy Airport. It was alleged that both men were traveling to Egypt and then on to Somalia, where they apparently planned to join al-Shabaab and "wage violent jihad."

According to a statement from the U.S. attorney in New Jersey, when Mohamed Mahmood Alessa and Carlos Eduardo Almonte arrived at the airport, a law enforcement team was waiting for them with arrest warrants in hand.

The criminal complaint, which laid out probable cause in the case, claimed that a tip in 2006 led an undercover officer with the New York Police Department Intelligence Division to take an interest in their activities. Meetings and conversations were recorded.

The feds said the men were preparing for jihad by squirreling away thousands of dollars, working out excessively, purchasing military gear, and buying plane tickets to Egypt. In the laundry list of allegations, the U.S. attorney said the men engaged "in paintball and other tactical training."

Reading between the lines, one can see that the feds believed the men's commitment to violence was escalating. Three weeks after the Fort Hood shooting, in late November 2009, one defendant allegedly confided to the other that a Daniel Pearl–style murder was a worthy tactic: "They only fear you when you have a gun and when you—when you start killing them, and when you—when you take their head, and you go like this, and you behead it on camera. . . . We'll start doing killing here, if I can't do it over there."

In the spring of 2010, one defendant said American troops would be in Somalia soon. He allegedly liked very much the idea of slaughtering Americans.

The criminal complaint suggested that the men were not sophisticated. The operation seemed haphazard. It was unclear whether the accused ever made direct contact with a Somali terrorist group before they bought their plane tickets.

The New York City police commissioner, Ray Kelly, told reporters that the men had traveled to Jordan three years earlier. They had tried to get into Iraq, but extremists had turned them down.

To complete the picture, these alleged "rec room" radicals played video and audio recordings for the undercover cop. The Internet tutorials were violent. They included lectures by al-Awlaki and videos from al-Shabaab. In February 2011, Alessa and Almonte pled guilty to conspiring to commit murder overseas on behalf of a terrorist organization.

Hammami, by all accounts, was quite the computer whiz

by the time his trek to East Africa was under way. In what is believed to be one of his early appearances, in 2007, obtained by the Middle East Media Research Institute (MEMRI), which monitors jihadist groups and their Web traffic, Hammami covered his face. Only his eyes, wide and earnest, could be seen as he addressed the camera in the Al Jazeera interview. The clip was brief, but Hammami made his point: "O Muslims of America, take into consideration the situation in Somalia. After fifteen years of chaos, and oppressive rule by the American-backed warlords, your brothers stood up and established peace and justice in this land."

The narrator identified Hammami as "Abu Monsour," an American instructor for the Islamic Courts Union, whose fighters want to build a Muslim state in East Africa. With his face still obscured, Hammami was shown building and testing what was described as a large bomb on the battlefield.

Hammami's journey to Somalia, like the stories of other digital jihadists, was the outcome of an evolution. Each step brought him closer to a more radical way of thinking. The idea of jihad was like a drug. Once hooked, he could never get enough.

By the spring of 2009, Hammami was no longer afraid to show his face. It was a sign of his commitment. It was also a sign that the Daphne, Alabama, native felt untouchable in East Africa.

In the video, obtained by MEMRI, Hammami was in the wilds of Somalia. It was pure propaganda. Like a wise father, Hammami counseled his fighters as they readied for an assault on the Ethiopian and Somali fighters who backed a secular government. The young man from Alabama, not even thirty, was fixated on an Islamic state. Known as "Amriki," which translated simply as "the American," he spoke in hushed tones: "Even though we're not seeing the enemy right at this moment— the enemy is very near, and if we hear that the enemy is moving, Allah willing, we'll be able to go and meet him."

What followed was an extraordinary reference to his American past. It suggested other Western recruits were along for the ride. "So the only reason we're staying here, away from your families, away from the cities, away from ice, candy bars, all these other things—is because we're waiting to meet with the enemy."

Once Hammami's lecture was complete, the young fighters didn't ride off into the sunset. They made their way into the rough terrain with a rap sound track in the background. It appeared Hammami was not only a fighter, but an aspiring performer and musician. The video showed that Hammami would adapt Western marketing to promote his war message.

Three months later, in July 2009, a new tape from Hammami showed that his star was on the rise. The message, which included a still photo of Hammami on the right, with a microphone pictured on the left, directly attacked President Obama. The format was reminiscent of the old Bin Laden tapes. It was no accident.

That summer, President Obama's speech from Cairo to the Muslim world was meant to open a new dialogue.

But Hammami's rebuttal to the president was not conciliatory. In this transcription by MEMRI, Hammami was stern: "We cannot and shall not extend our hands. Rather, we shall extend to you our swords until you leave our lands."

Hammami's statements were bold: "Let this not come as a surprise to those who were mesmerized by Obama's speech in Cairo. Our positions—both the American position and the position of the mujahideen—have not changed in the least. All that has changed is the way in which the position is being presented. The Prophet, peace be upon him, has already informed us of the power of speech. When he said, indeed in speech, there is a form of magic."

Then it got personal. "This magic of charisma is what lifted Obama to the global stage and what caused him to become the first African-American president. However, this power of conveyance and magical charisma has not changed the reality of the American goals. And it has not caused any success for America, economically or militarily."

Hammami showed no respect for or deference to the American president. He used his last name only. Mr. Obama's predecessor was also slighted. "But one very important change must be noted. Which is the change in the way America addresses the Muslims. The cowboy flavor has melted away. And instead we have a new apologetic and humble approach which seeks to find sympathetic people from within the Muslim world to spread the teachings of democracy by deceit instead of destruction."

The jihadist videos, especially those by Americans, told our team two things: how the message was evolving and how the messenger saw himself. By the spring of 2010, with the release of another video, Hammami was clearly a front man for the al Qaeda affiliate. He saw himself as an elder statesman. The tape felt like the final stage of his evolution from high school sweetheart to battlefield leader.

Called "Festival for the Children of the Martyrs," it opened with a video montage. A young boy, perhaps no more than five, was playing with a gun. But his smiling face took on a sinister expression when the video of a young man, presumed to be his dead father, flashed across the screen. The father, who was practicing with an automatic weapon on the beach, smiled periodically for the camera as the wind blew strongly against his chest. He wore a white baseball cap backward as he pulled the trigger.

The concept pulled at the heartstrings. In the video, bearing the al Qaeda logo, a golden trademark in the lower right-hand corner, Hammami called on followers of al Qaeda in Somalia to rise up and care for the children of the martyrs. It was impossible to know whether the story line was true or staged.

Though these videos were dramatic, it took—as Charlie Allen rightly pointed out—more than a video or a sermon for these Americans to cross the threshold to violence. Allen believed that often an encounter with a charismatic individual pushed them over the edge.

It was debatable when and where al-Awlaki crossed the threshold to violence. Allen felt it was in San Diego at the al-Rabat Mosque. It was there, in a modest ranch-style building, that al-Awlaki realized his power over the young, saw his ability to draw them in. He learned how to reach those under thirty who were not sure of their own identity. It was the same mosque where al-Awlaki met regularly with two of the 9/11 hijackers.

San Diego
Gas Lamp Quarter
February 9, 2010
1600 hours

I am on Facebook looking for an acquaintance, a onetime intelligence asset for the FBI. My gut tells me he can help with al-Awlaki.

I e-mail him, and within a day I have a response.

I first met Jim Moore (not his real name) in 2005. A fair-haired, blue-eyed convert to Islam, Moore is matter-of-fact about his past. His mother was into drugs. She died young under mysterious circumstances. He says his father was never on the scene. In his early teens, Moore converted to Islam. He went hard-core. There is still nothing halfway about the man, now thirty-six years old.

Tall and buff, Moore proudly explains how he lost a leg fighting the Russians in Chechnya. In the 1990s, he was elsewhere, fighting the good fight on behalf of other Muslims. He says he is a true believer.

At this stage of the Fox investigation, we know the alleged Fort Hood shooter, Major Nidal Hasan, sent at least eighteen e-mails to al-Awlaki. The cleric responded only a handful of times. It was very much Hasan pursuing the cleric. In one e-mail, Hasan asked al-Awlaki to give out prizes for a scholarship event. The cleric apparently declined, because he didn't visit the United States anymore.

The possible connection between Moore and al-Awlaki comes to me one morning as I run along the Potomac River. Moore is still plugged in, I say to myself. He will have the answers.

When Moore and I connect, the conversation is easy. Moore fills me in on a prison stint and a recent job working security for a reality television show. As we talk about al-Awlaki and his lectures at al-Rabat, it seems to ring a bell. Moore says he remembers a thin guy with dark hair and glasses. "No shit! Not that guy Anwar!" Moore exclaims over the phone. "That's the guy whose ass we [the U.S. government] tried to blow up in December. What a trip!"

Moore is referring to a cruise missile attack in December 2009. Amnesty International, the London-based human rights group, claimed that fifty-five were killed in the strike, including at least forty civilians. The exact circumstances of the strike are not public, but based on conversations in Washington, it is clear to me that al-Awlaki and leaders of al Qaeda in Yemen were the intended targets.

Moore says he sometimes sat near al-Awlaki at the mosque. He describes al-Awlaki's tight clique of friends and refers to him as the kind of guy who talks big but never gets his hands dirty. He leaves that to others.

We agree to meet in downtown San Diego at the U.S. Grant, an old-style hotel built a century ago. Moore will do an interview for the Fox investigation, but on his terms. We must conceal his identity. In return, he will take us on a driving tour of al-Awlaki's old neighborhood.

In a basement conference room, the interview is ready to go. Moore says he is in a lot of pain. He is chewing painkillers like gum and sucking on a Pepsi.

The lighting is moody. The room is hot. We begin with the basics.

"Tell us a little bit about al-Awlaki. What did he look like in those days?"

"This guy was small in stature, scrawny." Even in silhouette, Moore is uncomfortable talking about the cleric. He says he is worried there will be blowback once our investigation is broadcast.

"He sort of creeped you out?"

"Yeah," he answers.

I push Moore. One-word responses won't cut it for television.

"When he preached in the mosque, did he have a command-ing personality?" I ask.

Moore finally opens up. "Hate to use played-out words, but yes, yes, he was charismatic. I guess you could say some of the more susceptible members that might be listening to him were attracted to that charisma."

We show Moore some of al-Awlaki's most recent videos. We want to gauge how the cleric's image is evolving. Specifi-cally, how is the American marketing himself to his new digital followers?

We take Moore upstairs to one of our hotel rooms, which functions as a makeshift office. The sun is dropping. The af-ternoon light is drifting away. Moore sits next to me. Close to me, in fact. We are friends in the way reporters and their con-tacts can become friends. On the one hand, we don't quite trust them. On the other hand, we worry about their safety.

Our senior producer, Greg Johnson, nods his head. Johnson is the kind of field producer who flies into places most people with common sense are flying out of. The tape is rolling. Moore leans toward the computer and starts laughing—not the reac-tion I am expecting. Al-Awlaki's image floats across the screen: he wears a traditional tribal sword tucked into his belt. He looks like a brave and seasoned warrior.

Without hesitation, Moore says the cleric is a fake. "Is he sleeping on the ground? You know? Are the rocks and stones his pillows? I mean, come on, I think he's probably leading a fairly comfortable life. Kind of like an armchair quarter-back, praising other people for this or that, but yet he doesn't want to get involved in it himself." He shifts his weight in the chair. "If you feel strongly about it"—Moore is talking about protecting other Muslims as a religious duty—"if that's what you think you should be doing, then go out there and do it, you know?"

And while al-Awlaki was quick to praise the Fort Hood attack, Moore says the vast majority of Muslims he knows are condemning the attack. "I mean, just myself, I have about, probably ten friends, I've never met them in person, that I speak with on the Internet, that are, you know, blue-eyed, blond-haired Americans, that are either in Iraq or Afghanistan, and they are also Muslims."

Of his online soldier friends, Moore says, "They're out there fighting the bad guys, quote, unquote, and they're Muslims. They're not coming back to base and, you know, killing their brothers."

As Moore's anger rises, his observations become sharp and clear. He says there is no problem being Muslim and being an American. "Maybe some of the media want to make it out to be that way, maybe some of the extremists, like al-Awlaki, or whatever his name is, want to make it out to be that way. But the point is that there is no conflict. If you're an American and you're a Muslim, it's just like if you're an American and you're a Christian or whatever, you know? You believe what you believe."

Moore figures al-Awlaki likes the attention, even if he is praising cowardly acts like the massacre at Fort Hood.

Moore keeps his end of the deal and takes us on a tour of al-Awlaki's old neighborhood. Moore gets behind the wheel of our black SUV rental car. I am on the passenger side. The crew are in the backseat. Moore reassures us that driving with one leg is no problem.

"This is East San Diego," he says. Moore provides a running commentary as we weave through the traffic. "This is, like, the ghetto."

"Where are we right now?" The car is making a turn onto a major thoroughfare.

"We're about to hit El Cajon Boulevard. Which apparently somebody found very entertaining." There is sarcasm in Moore's voice.

Moore is referring to al-Awlaki's double life in San Diego. According to our reporting for the Fox investigation, al-Awlaki was picked up in San Diego and in Washington, D.C., for soliciting prostitutes. In a separate interview, a former FBI agent confirmed another disturbing incident: al-Awlaki was hauled in for loitering around a school.

Moore is taken aback. Al-Awlaki's extracurricular activities are more than he can stomach. As the imam, Moore says, al-Awlaki led prayers. He set himself above the others.

"Why would you be arrested for tutoring children?" Moore's rhetorical question hangs in the air.

"So it was obviously for another reason. If that's true, in an Islamic country, you would have, he would have his head chopped off."

. . .

One defect seemed to run through the lives of many successful and wannabe terrorists. We coined the term "sexual frenzy" for our project. You could say the promise of martyrdom and the fabled virgins was like a get-out-of-jail-free card. There was no problem sinning today when paradise was guaranteed tomorrow.

A month before the Fort Hood attack, the alleged shooter, Major Nidal Hasan, seemed to enter this sexual frenzy, during which he spent evenings at the Starz strip club just off base.

According to one dancer, who went by the stage name Paige,

Hasan was a recent and frequent customer. She said the Army major was respectful. He wasn't rowdy like other clients. He paid $50 for a lap dance in one of the club's private rooms, a week before the shooting, on both October 29 and October 30. He was a generous tipper.

The 9/11 hijackers were no strangers to strippers in the months before the attack. Right after 9/11 it was reported that at least five of the men, including the ringleader, Mohammed Atta, sampled the entertainment in Las Vegas. Some of the strippers said the group was polite. They were light drinkers.

What attracted the group to Las Vegas was unknown. It was an easy destination to reach. It had a transient population where foreign visitors would go unnoticed. A San Francisco newspaper reported that some of the hijackers made at least six trips to Sin City.

A recently declassified document presented a bizarre addition to the narrative. It also tied in al-Awlaki.

Omar al-Bayoumi was a Saudi. His was not a household name, but a search of the 9/11 Commission Report showed that the Saudi was worthy of further investigation by our team. As al-Bayoumi told the story, he was from San Diego and just happened to be in a Culver City, California, restaurant on the very day two hijackers, al-Hazmi and al-Mihdhar, showed up.

Al-Bayoumi and his traveling buddy told investigators they came to the Los Angeles area to sort out a visa issue. Al-Bayoumi also needed to pick up some papers at the Saudi consulate.

Investigators remained on the fence about the chance meeting. They wrote, "We do not know whether the lunch encounter occurred by chance or design. We know about it because Bayoumi told law enforcement that it happened."

At the time, al-Bayoumi, then forty-two, was a business student, enrolled in a professional improvement course sponsored by the Saudis' civil aviation authority. He met the two hijackers on February 1, 2000; less than a week later, they would show up at the Islamic Center of San Diego looking for him.

Al-Bayoumi, described by the 9/11 Commission as an outgoing and devout Muslim, helped the men find an apartment. He helped the hijackers, who did not speak or write much if any English, fill out the lease application, and he cosigned the agreement. He even helped the men open a bank account when the real estate agent would not accept cash. The initial deposit, nearly $10,000, was given to them by Khalid Sheikh Mohammed. And it appeared al-Bayoumi loaned his phone to the hijackers. An FBI agent would later report that four calls were made to al-Awlaki on February 4, 2000.

Al-Bayoumi was known to enjoy a good party. Shortly after the two hijackers moved into their apartment, which remained almost bare because they brought few possessions with them, the Saudi held a party with about twenty friends, one of whom videotaped the event for posterity. That apparently made the hijackers nervous. They spent most of the party by themselves, away from the camera.

Al-Bayoumi would later tell investigators that he didn't like the hijackers much either. In October 2003, al-Bayoumi met with senior members of the 9/11 Commission staff for nearly five hours. A footnote on a recently declassified "Memorandum for the Record" indicates that the session was interrupted only by a "multi-course dinner" hosted by a Saudi colonel.

The document was first obtained by intelwire.com, a clearinghouse for terrorism news and hard-to-obtain documents. It was generously shared with our Fox investigative team. It says,

"According to OAB [Omar al-Bayoumi], he was neighbors with NAH [Nawaf al-Hazmi] and KAM [Khalid al-Mihdhar] for only a few days and rarely saw them. An incident in which he and his son saw them roughhousing with each other made OAB very uncomfortable, and after that he no longer particularly wished to associate with them."

When asked what "roughhousing" meant, one of the 9/11 investigators said it was hard to know whether the hijackers' behavior might be appropriate in their circle. The men were grappling with each other. They were battled-trained in the Afghan camps.

It was impossible to understand the physical and cultural cues that upset al-Bayoumi. Asked if the incident had a sexual undertone, the investigator could not say.

Was the roughhousing a trial run to overcome the pilots in the cockpits, or something more? No conclusions can be reached, because the two primary witnesses, two of the five hijackers on Flight 77, are dead. However, a former FBI agent, who was a supervisor on the Arabian Peninsula squad after 9/11, said it was not uncommon for terrorists to engage in abnormal sexual behavior.

When we met Brian Weidner, at a hotel in Georgetown, he was a likable guy right off the bat. Retired now for a few years, he relished discussing the old days as an investigator. He seemed to miss the chase.

One of Weidner's biggest cases was that of the Institute of Islamic and Arabic Sciences in America (IIASA) in Fairfax, Virginia, a few miles from the nation's capital. Weidner maintained that radical views were taught at the institute, set up by Saudi prince Bandar in 1998. He said it encouraged young Americans to buy into extremist thinking. In 2004, the institute was raided by Homeland Security, the IRS, and FBI agents, and it was eventually shut down.

Weidner was matter-of-fact about the double life many of these terrorists led. The former FBI agent's take was consistent with the statements of a senior official with the national counterterrorism center who said it was common to pick up suspects and find 90 percent of their hard drives were porn. "Traditional Islam, especially Salafist Islam, is significantly sexually repressive," Weidner said. "Historically, when we see sexually repressive environments, the people do strange things."

Weidner knew al-Awlaki from the IIASA case. The cleric attended classes at the institute. Weidner was also familiar with al-Awlaki's double life. He knew about three incidents in San Diego: the two pickups for soliciting prostitutes, and the one for loitering around a school.

Weidner also knew about another incident that caught the FBI's attention. Weidner said al-Awlaki was caught soliciting a young girl in Washington, D.C. While nothing ever really disappears from government files, D.C. authorities claimed that al-Awlaki's police record was destroyed years ago. It was simply an old case that was never prosecuted. The girl's age remained a mystery. But based on Weidner's statements, it appeared she was a minor.

Al-Awlaki apparently took the girl from D.C. to Virginia, where he lived and worked. It was a relatively short drive. Weidner said the feds considered charging al-Awlaki under the Mann Act. Passed at the turn of the last century, the law was designed to stop men from taking underage girls across state lines for sex. The law was more commonly used to bring cases against pimps and indiscreet celebrities.

Weidner said the charge was eventually dropped. He didn't

know why, and no official wanted to talk about it. In similar cases, it was not uncommon for the prostitute, even those under sixteen, to get cold feet and decline to testify.

Based on al-Awlaki's Web lectures and sermons, he was the poster boy for a double life. On the one hand, he espoused the virtues and the carnal pleasures that await the martyrs in paradise. On the other hand, he spoke openly about his disgust for procreation on earth.

In both cities, he held important leadership positions at the mosque. He had a young wife and a family. Yet, in his off time, in Virginia and in San Diego, al-Awlaki let off steam in inappropriate ways.

Moore, who knew al-Awlaki at the al-Rabat Mosque in San Diego, was offended when he learned about the multiple prostitution violations. He spoke with more than a hint of sarcasm.

Years before, Moore said, a Muslim commander in the war between the Russians and the Chechens refused to lead prayers because of his faults. Moore implied that the commander was a holier and more devout man than al-Awlaki. "He [the commander] would not lead his soldiers in prayer, which would make him an imam, at that time," said Moore. "There's a verse in the Koran that says if you lead others in prayer, on the day of judgment you will be held more accountable for your sins. . . . So, now that's something respectable. He's basically saying I'm not perfect."

Moore was visibly angry. Even in silhouette for our interview, the tension was palpable. He offered this vivid image of al-Awlaki. It was not one readily found on the Web or in his lectures. "You have this guy who's actively sitting there telling people, you know, this is how you should conduct your affairs. . . . If that's the case he should also say that, you know, while you're going down El Cajon Boulevard, on this side of the street they have the more expensive prostitutes, and this side they have the cheaper ones."

Moore paused. "I mean, he might as well include that in his speech, because it all fits in with how to run your life. Right?"

. . .

After 9/11, U.S. officials watched as plots unfolded across Europe. On March 11, 2004, a series of coordinated attacks on the commuter network in Madrid, Spain, killed 191 and injured more than 1,800. Inspired by al Qaeda, a cell of Spaniards and North Africans used backpacks laden with explosives to hit four trains within a fifteen-minute time frame during the morning rush hour. A year later, on July 7, 2005, a group of young British men, three of them of Pakistani descent, carried similar devices onto the London Underground and buses. Fifty-six were killed and another seven hundred were injured.

In Washington, there was alarm mixed with a growing sense of smugness that the homegrown terrorist was a European phenomenon and not our problem. The rationale was that the U.S. Muslim population was not at risk. America's melting pot was at work and it provided some insulation. But a few years later, the warning signs seemed to be everywhere.

Now a piece of advice from a senior FBI agent made sense to me. It was important, the agent said, to look not only at the leader but also at his followers. The followers will tell you the profile. Paying attention to them will show who is buying into the message.

In 2009, the Senate Homeland Security Committee was told that there had been eight homegrown plots and two successful attacks in the United States. The successful attacks included the mass shooting at Fort Hood and an attack on the military recruiting center in Little Rock, Arkansas. The eight plots were a significant jump over previous years. Both of the successful attacks had loose connections to al-Awlaki.

Al-Awlaki was connected to Fort Hood through the Hasan e-mails. The Arkansas case was more complex. But with some digging, we established the connection to al-Awlaki's group in Yemen.

Carlos Bledsoe, also known as Abdulhakim Mujahid Muhammad, was arrested for a drive-by shooting at the Little Rock, Arkansas, military recruitment center that killed one soldier and injured another. In an FBI press release, Bledsoe was accused of murder and attempted murder.

Not long after his arrest, Bledsoe wrote a letter to the court. He claimed to be a member of al Qaeda in the Arabian Peninsula, the same al Qaeda affiliate tied to al-Awlaki and the underwear bomber. In his handwritten letter to the judge, Bledsoe stated:

> I'm affiliated with Al-Qaeda in the Arabian Peninsula. Member of Abu Basir's Army. This was a Jihadi attack on infidel forces. That didn't go as plan. Flat out Truth. I plead to capital Murder, Attempt capital Murder and the other 10 counts without compulsion without Deals. . . . I wasn't insane or post traumatic nor was I forced to do this Act. Which I believe and it is justified according to Islamic Laws and the Islamic Religion. Jihad—to fight those who wage war on Islam and Muslims.

The more research we did, the more al-Awlaki and al Qaeda in Yemen cropped up. Every once in a while, a congressional report cuts through the political correctness and hits the nail on the head. One such report, titled "Al Qaeda in Yemen and Somalia: A Ticking Time Bomb," was the work of staffers for the well-respected Senate Foreign Relations Committee.

The "letter of transmittal" by Chairman John Kerry got right to the point. Kerry wrote that military and intelligence operations were putting pressure on al Qaeda in the tribal areas of Pakistan. Now, there was strong evidence that "hundreds— or perhaps even thousands—of fighters" were heading to more hospitable territory. Senator Kerry fingered Yemen and Somalia as well as North Africa and Southeast Asia. While the groups did not take their marching orders from al Qaeda's core leadership, they still shared the same goals: death, destruction, and the recruitment of American operatives.

A few simple lines confirmed that our investigation was onto something:

> These Americans are not necessarily of Arab or South Asian descent; they include individuals who converted to Islam in prison or elsewhere and were radicalized.

Based on expert testimony and briefings from senior U.S. government officials, every detail was like the piece of a giant puzzle that was starting to come together. The picture was unsettling.

> Law enforcement and intelligence officials told the Committee staff in interviews in December in Yemen . . . that as many as 36 American ex-convicts arrived in Yemen in the past year, ostensibly to study Arabic.

And while there were legitimate reasons to study Arabic in Yemen, investigators felt the ex-cons' claims were a cover story.

Some of the Americans had disappeared and are suspected of having gone to al Qaeda training camps in ungoverned portions of the impoverished country. Similar concerns are expressed about a smaller group of Americans who moved to Yemen, adopted a radical form of Islam, and married local women.

I stopped reading and looked up. It all seemed to be here.

Charlie Allen told me he'd informally analyzed the data. He did not believe that the propaganda, especially on the Internet, was effective on the vast majority of American Muslims. Allen said those who immigrated to the United States in the fifties and sixties had reconciled their faith with the American way of life. They were well educated and mainstream, and had no problem integrating their religion with American core values of human rights, self-determination, and democracy.

"I do believe we need to be more concerned, and this is my own theory just looking at the data," Allen said carefully. "Those who arrived here in the last ten or fifteen years I don't think are as well adjusted. I think they're more alienated. I think the Somali population is an example of that.

"The Somalis who came here, the first generation who were naturalized Americans, are not as adjusted . . . more alienated. They are congregated in a number of cities. Minneapolis–St. Paul. They're in Portland, Oregon; Portland, Maine; Nashville; San Diego; they're in other areas of the country."

Allen continued: "I do believe that we need to look hard

at those immigrants who've arrived here in the last ten, fifteen years from Muslim countries."

To me, it was another way of saying that those between sixteen and thirty are vulnerable. There was no obvious profile. The idea that America was immune from the homegrown threat was a misconception.

In the summer of 2010, al Qaeda in Yemen launched a new online magazine for a Western audience. It was a bold move, showing that the organization thought our ground was fertile for recruitment. Called *Inspire,* it was a lifestyle magazine for would-be jihadists along the lines of *Martha Stewart Living* or Oprah's *O* magazine.

It made such a splash that *Vanity Fair* described it this way: "Publishing powerhouse al-Qaeda has launched an English online magazine called *Inspire,* replete with all the bomb-making instructions and jihad-recruiting propaganda that traditional print journalism has traditionally shunned."

Anwar al-Awlaki had a featured piece in the first issue, "May Our Souls Be Sacrificed for You." The magazine's graphics were clean and crisp. I later learned that it was thought to be the work of another American, Samir Khan, who once ran a jihadist blog from his parents' basement in North Carolina. It was an online version of the type of magazine you could leaf through at the dentist's office. It felt so familiar. A scenic skyline of Chicago complete with the John Hancock Building graced one issue. That seemed like a deliberate dig at the president and his hometown, but it would turn out to be something more sinister.

The debut was not flawless. The magazine was posted in high- and medium-quality formats. Both files were corrupted, and this led some jihadists to post online messages that the PDFs contained spyware:

> WARNING: Dear brothers, visitors to the Al-Fallujah Islamic Forum: We warn you against downloading the PDF file to INSPIRE magazine from Al-Malahem Media Foundation. This file contains virus and spyware!!! We warn you against downloading this PDF file in [*sic*] any website or to trust any publications of this magazine as it is the work of the apostat hypocrit [*sic*] dogs who are trying to discredit the Mujahideens. So be AWARE, be AWARE may God protect you. Your brothers in the administration at the Al-Fallujah Islamic Forum.

The corrupted files led to what MEMRI described as a meltdown on the jihadist forums. "In conclusion, the sequence of events that began with the release of *Inspire* magazine ended in a major disaster for the online jihadi community. It is difficult to say with certainty whether the supposed virus in the magazine was responsible for the security breach, but the circumstantial evidence certainly points in that direction."

I felt myself constantly pulled back to the first issue. The mix of Western-style graphics and bloody content was intriguing. The last few pages were the most illuminating. Titled "O Allah, Free the Muslim Prisoners," it was a who's who of al-Awlaki's alleged followers. As I scanned the list, the names were familiar—Colleen LaRose, the Fort Dix Six, Umar Farouk Abdulmutallab, Nidal Hasan, and Faisal Shahzad. But it was the second-to-last page that stood out: "If you are interested in contributing to this magazine with any skills—be it writing, editing, designing or advice—you can contact us at any of the email addresses below." Included were accounts on Hotmail, Gmail, Yahoo!, and FastMail.

Jim Moore said that some members of al-Awlaki's San Diego mosque were susceptible to such messages. He said the cleric was destroying the reputations of Muslims and of Islam. "Him and his ilk . . . they're giving American Muslims a bad name," Moore said. "One of these days, maybe somebody's just going to get tired of him smearing an entire religion and an entire group of people within that religion." He paused. "You know, things happen."

At the time, I didn't read much into Moore's statement, but not long after *Fox News Reporting: The American Terrorist* was broadcast, we talked again. Moore wanted a favor. He wanted a hookup for overseas. His money situation was bad. He might be willing to work for the government again. He thought he could get close to al-Awlaki.

···

CHAPTER 3

SLIPPING THROUGH THE NET

Washington, D.C.
State Department
March 12, 2010

I t's not making any sense." I am sitting in the Fox News workspace at the State Department in Washington's Foggy Bottom. It is one of the few places where twenty-something Ivy Leaguers feel comfortable wearing bow ties.

The networks have modest workspaces off the briefing room. It is supposed to improve access. Reporters get more face time with State Department officials. They pick up secrets in the hallway.

But the American cleric's story is different. Even the mention of Anwar al-Awlaki's name brings silence and discouraging looks.

I've got to think strategically, I say to myself. I am working through the proper channels to secure an interview with the former Diplomatic Security agent who knows more about the cleric than anyone else.

Ray Fournier is an agent's agent. He is dedicated and kind. He never forgets the mission. He wears one lapel pin: it is a detective's shield with 9/11 engraved at the top. As we will later learn, the cleric is a black spot on Fournier's memory.

Diplomatic Security (DS) is the law enforcement branch of the State Department. Passport fraud was Fournier's specialty. He handled more than three hundred felony arrest warrants for passport fraud during his eighteen years at State. Only one case didn't stick.

That is the case Fournier and I need to talk about. Even though he is out of DS and his case file on al-Awlaki is closed, I still need permission from his old boss at State. And I need permission from Fournier's new boss at Homeland Security.

It shouldn't be hard, but then, every train wreck in TV news begins with the phrase "This will be a piece of cake."

There is no legitimate reason to block Fournier's interview. But my first approach to the press handlers at the State Department falls flat. In a series of curt e-mails and phone calls, our team is told there is no way the former agent can talk about al-Awlaki.

At home, after Jamie and Peter are in bed, I turn to my husband for advice. J.D. counsels persistence as he heads to the basement and the man cave. Most nights there is nothing he, like a lot of soldiers, enjoys more than a few video games to get "killing the bad guys" out of his system.

J.D. is right. It is time to kick the request upstairs to State Department spokesman P. J. Crowley.

After a routine briefing at State, I corner Crowley. In Washington media circles, it is common to hold the on-camera, on-the-record briefing first. A background briefing without cameras follows.

Crowley seems pretty straight-up. He tells me he has no problem with Fournier doing the Fox interview. Reading between the lines, my assessment is that Crowley thinks blocking the interview would not be consistent with the Obama administration's stated goal of transparency.

I want to believe it's true. I need to believe it's true. But everything I am hearing from federal sources, where Fournier now works, is that Crowley is apparently against the interview. He is the one blocking it.

I decide to take Crowley at his word. After all, at the time he was the main spokesman for Secretary of State Hillary Clinton. He had earned the benefit of the doubt.

I begin typing.

3/12/10
Subject line: thanks!

Good to see you in person today at State.

Thank you for following up on our request. I am glad to hear the hang-up for the DS agent interview is not on your end. I will pursue it over at DHS.

Many thanks.
Catherine

It's a solid strategy. I hit the Send button. My next call is to the Homeland Security official Crowley identified as the problem party.

A few days later, I am in the greenroom at Fox. It is the holding pen for guests before they hit air. Many important deals are cut in the greenroom hallway. The conversations flow freely in this off-the-record environment.

I won't go into detail about my greenroom conversation and whom it was with, because of the ground rules. All you need to know is that I am skipping down the hallway after the meeting. Homeland Security officials insist Fournier can talk.

It seems to be a political calculation—another sign, critics would say, of the Obama administration's penchant to be constantly in campaign mode. The interview with the former State Department agent is not going to make Homeland Security secretary Janet Napolitano look bad. Fumbling the ball with al-Awlaki eight years ago was a Bush administration problem.

It is time to write the next e-mail to Crowley. I didn't get any response after my first e-mail, so I assume everything is cool.

3/18/2010 5:58p

PJ,

Thank you for following up on our request. I was glad to hear that the hang-up for the former DS agent interview is not on your end. As you suggested, I have connected with your DHS counterparts . . . who tell me they do not object to the interview either. I am very pleased.

I am now going to book Fournier for our documentary.

Many thanks for helping us resolve the issue,
Catherine

By late afternoon, I am e-mailing Fournier with the good news. Everyone says they are on board for the interview. Five days later, Fournier is on the phone. He says he's got the clearance he needs.

3/23/2010 11:18a
Subject line: re: interview approved.

Catherine,

Interview approved. One caveat. There can be no mention of my current employer or my current employment. They want me to be identified as a "former DS agent."

"When are you coming?" Fournier asks me on the phone later that day. His voice is relaxed and easy.

"I don't know. How about tomorrow? Are you available tomorrow?" Though he doesn't say anything, I sense Fournier is a little stunned. It is an odd request. But I have a strong feeling we need the interview in the can.

"Okay, sure." Fournier is accommodating. We agree to meet late afternoon, around four o'clock. My producer, Greg Johnson, and I are booked on the first flight out to San Diego the next morning.

As the plane taxis on the runway at Dulles, I slump down

in my seat and think about Fournier. He says al-Awlaki is a black spot on his memory, a thorn in his side. I need to understand why.

. . .

After 9/11, Anwar al-Awlaki was a high-priority target—a "tier-one target" in law-enforcement parlance—because of his known contacts with the hijackers. As we discussed earlier, the thirty-year-old cleric was interviewed at least four times by the FBI between September 15 and September 19, 2001.

That same month, September 2001, the cleric was also on the JTTF's radar. Fournier was assigned from Diplomatic Security to the JTTF unit in San Diego.

San Diego was a hotbed of terrorist activity. As we noted earlier, two of the hijackers went to al-Awlaki's al-Rabat Mosque. One of the men, Nawaf al-Hazmi, found temporary work at a nearby gas station.

According to the 9/11 Commission Report, the gas station was a logical choice. Some of al-Hazmi's friends worked there, including Mohdar Abdullah.

Mohdar Abdullah was a Yemeni national. Investigators believe he drove al-Hazmi and Khalid al-Mihdhar, the two hijackers who spoke virtually no English, from Los Angeles to San Diego and al-Awlaki's mosque. The 9/11 Commission Report said he was "perfectly suited" to help the hijackers because he was fluent in English and Arabic.

As we will later see, Abdullah, al-Awlaki, and a Jordanian, Eyad al-Rababah, may be the missing links in the 9/11 conspiracy. New evidence raises a simple question: Were the three men part of a support cell to facilitate the plot? If true, it will rewrite history and our understanding of the worst terrorist attack on American soil.

At the JTTF in the fall of 2001, Fournier's job was finding the hijackers' associates. The feds were hungry for leads. On most mornings, a new list of names came down from the FBI. Each name had several permutations. Sometimes new names surfaced overnight. Fournier's job, and that of the other agents, was to run down the details by four o'clock the same day.

It wasn't a perfect world, where answers came quickly. The lists were complicated and the work was relentless. The briefings and the digging went on for months.

"I had a file with several hundred names generated by the JTTF," Fournier said. But of all the names he was tasked with, Anwar al-Awlaki stood out.

"I was approached by a supervisor within the FBI at JTTF along with an agent from Immigration and Naturalization. And we were told, this person is of importance, he was known to have associations with al-Mihdhar and al-Hazmi. We were told to look at the statutory authority within our various organizations, and apply those capabilities to Anwar al-Awlaki."

In simple terms, Fournier and his counterparts were instructed to find a reason to pick up the cleric.

Like all good investigators, Fournier began with the low-hanging fruit. At the time, the JTTF believed that al-Awlaki was a Yemeni national who had illegally obtained a U.S. passport or committed visa fraud. So Fournier traveled to New Mexico, al-Awlaki's purported birthplace. A thorough search at the Bureau of Vital Statistics showed that the cleric was, in fact, born there.

Fournier kept digging. He sensed that al-Awlaki, like all good terrorists, was using our system against us. When al-

Awlaki was ready for college in 1990, he wanted to return to the United States. From what Fournier could work out, he walked into the U.S. embassy in the Yemeni capital of Sana'a and applied for a J-1 visa. Fournier was puzzled. The J-1 visa was reserved for foreign exchange visitors, not American citizens.

Al-Awlaki entered the United States on June 5, 1990, on an Exchange Visitor (J-1) visa. His ultimate destination was Colorado State University and its engineering program. Fournier started searching through all of the State Department records. To his surprise, he found that the American embassy in Yemen issued the cleric a U.S. passport in 1988 and a foreign student visa two years later. Fournier believed the J-1 visitor's visa was placed in al-Awlaki's Yemeni passport. He was a dual national.

"How can that happen?" I asked.

"There was no cross-pollination of the databases. So it could have been overlooked." Fournier paused. "Clearly, it was overlooked."

Fournier concluded that al-Awlaki was gaming the system. He lied about his nationality to get a slice of a lucrative scholarship, through the U.S. State Department. The lie paid off. Using his Yemeni passport, Awlaki pocketed $20,000 in scholarship money paid for by the U.S. taxpayer. And here's the kicker: al-Awlaki would never have qualified for the scholarship money as an American citizen.

Much to Fournier's disappointment, the statute of limitations had run out on the foreign-student scam. Al-Awlaki made several false statements to get the J-1 visa and the scholarship money, but the lies were made in 1990 or earlier. A decade later, al-Awlaki's bad behavior slipped through the net. It was a pattern that would repeat itself, with profound consequences.

Fournier didn't give up. Next, he scrutinized al-Awlaki's

Social Security application. Al-Awlaki was fastidious about his records. On June 5, 1990, he landed in Chicago, on his way to Fort Collins, Colorado. The next day, despite the brutal jet lag, al-Awlaki headed straight for the Social Security Administration.

On the SSN application, he claimed he was born in Yemen. According to Fournier, he provided his Yemeni passport and his J-1 visa as proof. His Social Security number was issued on June 8, 1990, just three days after he entered the country as a bogus foreign student.

Fournier confirmed that al-Awlaki did work in college. By all accounts, the job was typical student stuff, pushing paper for school administrators.

There wasn't another reason to look at the cleric until three years later. In 1993, he renewed his U.S. passport. You'll remember, he had got a U.S. passport at the American embassy in Yemen five years earlier. He was sixteen at the time.

On his passport renewal, November 18, 1993, Awlaki presented his valid birth certificate from Las Cruces, New Mexico, where he was born in April 1971. Unfortunately for al-Awlaki, in the upper right corner of the passport application, he used the Social Security number he had fraudulently obtained three years earlier. Using the bogus Social Security number meant the passport application was now a continuation of the fraud.

Fournier had finally caught a break. Al-Awlaki renewed his passport in 1993. It was now only the spring of 2002. The statute of limitations for passport fraud was ten years. So the clock was still ticking: the San Diego JTTF had another year before the statute of limitations ran out and al-Awlaki was off the hook again.

"So you are looking at this paperwork and you are saying, 'I think I have got him.'" I could feel the energy rise in the room.

"Absolutely, there was no doubt we had him," Fournier replied. He was confident the charge would stick even though his investigation was creative. Fourier was looking for any opening. "I am confident this violation of the law applies to him." Fournier said his supervisors at the JTTF in San Diego were equally ecstatic. "There was a jubilation that a charge—a valid felony charge, absolutely valid—would apply to Anwar al-Awlaki."

Fournier said the time to do the legwork was now (spring of 2002), while the cleric was out of the country. While the timeline was sketchy, he believed that al-Awlaki had left for Yemen because the heat was on.

Fournier wanted an arrest warrant ready in case the cleric returned to the country. All of the evidence was compiled in an affidavit of probable cause. It laid out the case against al-Awlaki. It justified the arrest to a federal court of law.

Key phrases in the eight-year-old document jumped out at me. There were also multiple spellings of his name.

On the cover page it read simply: "United States of America Vs. Anwar Nasser Aulaqi."

In the right-hand margin: "Warrant for Arrest Case Number 02-1146m."

"You are hereby commanded to arrest Anwar Nasswer [sic] Aulaqi and bring him forthwith to the nearest magistrate to answer a . . ."

The box was checked by "Complaint."

There was only one count. It was underlined in thick black ink: <u>COUNT 1</u>

On or about November 18, 1993, in the State and District of Colorado, ANWAR NASSER AULAQI, a/k/a Anwar Nasser Abdulla Aulaqi . . . filled out and presented a form DSP-11, Application for United States Passport, falsely and fraudulently and knowingly using a social security number (521-77-7121) that he had obtained by fraud, all in violation of Title 18, United States Code, Section 1542.

A U.S. magistrate in Denver, Colorado, signed it. The date was handwritten. It was June 17, 2002, at 10:25 a.m. It was slightly crooked on the page.

At the time the arrest warrant was drawn up, al-Awlaki was thirty-one years old. The penalty for his lies was "NMT"—shorthand for "not more than"—ten years' imprisonment, a fine of NMT $250,000, or both.

At least that would go some way to paying back the scholarship money.

The final section of the affidavit caught my attention. The government had the option of seeking detention or allowing the defendant to go free, presumably on bail. A bold X marked the line "will seek detention in this case": another piece of evidence confirming Fournier's claim that the warrant was issued so that al-Awlaki could be charged and held in custody.

Fournier said that while most DS files were relatively thin, al-Awlaki's passport file was an inch and a half thick. This file was stuffed with two passport applications, the Social Security fraud paperwork, and al-Awlaki's booking photos for picking up hookers in San Diego.

Months of work had finally paid off. An arrest warrant meant the net was in place. Now it was time to wait.

Asked if securing the warrant had any special significance,

once again, Fournier was an agent's agent. "Oh, absolutely. To be able to serve the taxpayer, especially so soon after an emotionally devastating event such as 9/11."

Fournier paused. He collected himself and his thoughts.

"It was truly a privilege to have the opportunity to be able to write up such a strong statement of facts against an individual who clearly had very close ties to at least two of the San Diego–based terrorists, if not the third one in Virginia—"

"You were confident that it would stick, this case would stick?" I asked, interrupting Fournier.

"One hundred percent," Fournier responded. "Absolutely. Without a doubt."

Little did Fournier know that within four months, his hard work and that of his colleagues at the JTTF would unravel under the most mysterious of circumstances.

Fox News Channel
400 North Capitol Street NW
Washington, D.C.
March 22, 2010

I am looking at three pages of customs documents. They are a faded old printout. The words and letters are slightly irregular.

I know the documents are important, so I reach into my black vinyl backpack and pull out a pair of drugstore reading glasses. I finally sucked up my pride over the weekend and bought them at the military commissary at Bolling Air Force Base. The presidential helicopters are based just north of there, at Anacostia Naval Station.

I go there a lot with the kids, especially when my husband is deployed. As we drive through the gate in the old red

Volkswagen—top down—I show my military ID. I jokingly call it the "chattel card" because it grants military spouses limited privileges on base.

It always breaks my heart when five-year-old Jamie salutes the guards as we drive through. J.D. taught him the proper salute. The hand position and arm angle are important, J.D. said. I want our country to be free of this terrorist menace. I don't want Jamie or Peter to face war in the future.

The customs documents are not my discovery. Author Paul Sperry was the first to write about al-Awlaki's peculiar return to the United States on October 10, 2002. Sperry tells me the documents were leaked to him, adding that the leak led to an aggressive internal investigation at Homeland Security for the source. As a result, Sperry says, some of his contacts were harassed.

In his books, *Infiltration: How Muslim Spies and Subversives Have Penetrated Washington* and *Muslim Mafia: Inside the Secret Underworld That's Conspiring to Islamize America,* Sperry has shown a keen interest in the cleric. He generously shares the information with our Fox investigative team.

I put on my drugstore reading glasses. I like them. They are not *too* Sarah Palin. I scan the upper left-hand corner of the page, where the date is clearly marked: "10/10/2002." The airport is JFK International.

The last name is typed "Aulaqi." First name is listed as "Anwar." The date of birth matches up with our reporting: "04211971." There is no question. It is the cleric.

Reading such a document is second nature to customs agents, but the notations are like a foreign language to me, so I go slowly. From what I can make out, there was a secondary inspection for al-Awlaki and his family at JFK. Their bags were searched. Another notation suggests that the cleric was coming off an overnight flight from Saudi Arabia.

There is one note that catches my eye even though I don't yet fully understand its gravity. At 0615, the notification process began. At 0640 Special Agent Ammerman of the FBI was called. His cell phone was apparently not working. It was so early in the morning, I wonder if it was turned off.

This makes me pause. I will have to come back to the name Ammerman. It is familiar but I can't remember why.

At 0645 a customs agent was called to get another telephone number for Agent Ammerman. At approximately 0740, a customs agent listed as "S/A Kane" made a startling call to inspectors. Kane was "NOTIFYING US [the customs officers who detained al-Awlaki] THE WARRANT ISSUED BY THE STATE DEPT. HAD BEEN PULLED BACK."

From what I can make out, a feverish round of phone calls ensued. The documents say that all relevant calls were made. At 0920 that same morning, the American cleric, who was then tied to at least three successful or attempted attacks on U.S. soil, was released from federal custody and sent on his way.

And the kicker, according to Sperry's documents, is that al-Awlaki was thanked for his patience and given a comment card: "09:20 PASSENGERS RELEASED WITH THANKS FOR THEIR PATIENS [*sic*] AND GIVEN THE COMMENT CARD. PAX ESCORTED TO SAUDIA REP IN ORDER TO CONTINUE WITH THEIR FLIGHT TO WASH. DC."

A lot of things are bothering me now. For one, federal agents held the cleric for almost three hours at JFK. He was safely in the net. There was no way out for al-Awlaki, until we let him walk away.

The name Ammerman is bothering me too because I know it, but I don't know how. I make a quick call to a longtime lawyer at Guantánamo Bay, Edward MacMahon Jr., whom I first met in the trial of Zacarias Moussaoui, the so-called twentieth hijacker. He wasn't, but like a lot of media shorthand, the moniker stuck. Moussaoui was apparently too hapless, talkative, and unreliable to earn the trust of al Qaeda senior leadership and the hijackers.

I call MacMahon. We keep the idle chitchat to a minimum. The following is our conversation, as best I can recall.

"Ed, do you recognize this name, an FBI Agent Wade Ammerman?"

"[Expletive] Wade Ammerman. You bet I know him. Catherine, I told you when you started this project that Awlaki showed up in Ali's case."

Ali is MacMahon's onetime client Ali al-Timimi. Al-Timimi was convicted by a federal court in Virginia of inciting jihad against the United States in April 2005. MacMahon says al-Awlaki showed up at al-Timimi's house in the fall of 2002 and that the visit was unannounced. "I'll get Michele to send you the documents." Ed hangs up quickly. Michele is Ed's secretary. Of course, she is much more than that. All good defense attorneys need strong backup. Michele is like a deep bench.

After scanning the court documents, I put them down on the desk. The timing of the alleged visit by al-Awlaki to al-Timimi's house in Virginia makes me uneasy. The fall of 2002 is when al-Awlaki returned to the United States.

I go back to the customs log. It shows that at 0920 al-Awlaki was escorted to his connecting flight. The destination was Washington, D.C. MacMahon tells me that Ammerman was the FBI's number one or number two agent in the al-Timimi case. Ammerman was also the agent who told customs to let the cleric go at JFK. Agent Ammerman is the connection.

MacMahon takes me further into the al-Timimi case. He says his client had no idea who the cleric was when he showed up in Northern Virginia. "Anwar Awlaki was brought to Ali Timimi's house by a person named Nabil Garbeih, who turned out to be a government witness against Timimi."

According to his client and what's written in the court pleadings, MacMahon says al-Awlaki made a bizarre request. "Awlaki tried to get Ali to help him recruit young American Muslims to go join the jihad and that Timimi sent him out of the house and sent him away."

MacMahon is now irate. According to the court pleadings, al-Timimi believed al-Awlaki was wired. Their conversation was being recorded. MacMahon asked the court for any tapes or debriefing notes. The response from prosecutors was curt: "Al-Timimi seeks the Court to order the government to produce tapes he suggests that Aulaqi made while visiting Al-Timimi. We are aware of no authority for this request."

At that time, al-Timimi's defense attorney didn't know about al-Awlaki's connection to the FBI agent or about his mysterious return to the United States. During the discovery process, MacMahon said, the al-Awlaki arrest warrant was never provided to the defense. It came to his attention only because of our investigation.

"The idea that Anwar Awlaki, connected to the 9/11 hijackers, is just going to be allowed into the United States, you know, to travel around, maybe go shopping, whatever someone like Mr. Awlaki does during the day, is preposterous to me," MacMahon exclaimed.

• • •

By the summer and early fall of 2002, Diplomatic Security agent Ray Fournier was feeling pretty good. He thought his arrest warrant for al-Awlaki on passport fraud would stick. The feds could only hope that the cleric, who had been safely out of the country for months, would make the mistake of returning.

In the first week of October, Fournier got an unexpected and disturbing phone call. His counterpart in Denver said the U.S. attorney was having problems keeping the al-Awlaki arrest warrant active.

The warrant was issued in Colorado because the fraud was committed there. Fournier was dispatched to Denver by the State Department. On his way in from the airport, al-Awlaki and the passport fraud case were racing through his mind. Fournier felt confident that a recent decision by the United States Court of Appeals, Ninth Circuit, would bolster his case that the arrest warrant was solid.

In *U.S. vs. Hart*, the Ninth Circuit Court found that you cannot lie on a passport application. Period. It doesn't matter whether the lie was material. As one example, let's say you are an American citizen. Whether you are single or divorced won't affect your right to hold a U.S. passport. But if you lie on the application and claim to be divorced when you've never been married, the State Department can deny the application.

Fournier felt the case law was strongly on his side. In addition, al-Awlaki was a high-priority target. The JTTF in San Diego was not trying to create new case law. It was a creative way to pick up and hold a man who may have known about the 9/11 plot in advance.

The meeting in Denver lasted half an hour. It included Fournier; his Colorado counterpart in Diplomatic Security, Agent

Steven R. Click; and two representatives from the U.S. attorney's office, including Assistant U.S. Attorney David Gaouette.

Gaouette led the discussion. According to Fournier, he offered two reasons for pulling the warrant. Gaouette said the State Department would have issued al-Awlaki the passport because he was born here. Also, although al-Awlaki had fraudulently obtained his Social Security number, he had gone back and "corrected the record."

Our team would later learn that the second reason was pure spin. The fact that al-Awlaki lied to get a Social Security number in 1990 was not in dispute.

In 1996, once he was done with his studies at Colorado State and had used the $20,000 in scholarship money, al-Awlaki went back to the Social Security Administration. The office was not far from his new mosque in San Diego. This time, the cleric applied for a replacement card and used his true place of birth. In an extraordinary turn of events, the U.S. attorney claimed al-Awlaki had now "corrected the record."

Fournier said that U.S. Attorney David Gaouette did not want to hear any of his arguments. Though Fournier said he and the second agent assured Gaouette that al-Awlaki was a unique case, their appeals fell on deaf ears. Gaouette "was not interested in the results of the Ninth Circuit Court decision," and reading between the lines, Fournier suggested that higher powers were pulling the U.S. attorney's strings. "He was operating under other orders," Fournier said.

Our Fox investigative team was connecting the dots. We knew that the U.S. attorney seemed to go out of his way to vacate the arrest warrant, at a time when federal law enforcement feared a second wave of attacks. Young Muslim men across the country had been rounded up by federal authorities and held on material-witness warrants. Given that backdrop, why did the U.S. attorney seem to make excuses for al-Awlaki?

By now, we knew there was a connection between al-Awlaki's reentry into the United States and a senior FBI agent who was working another terrorism case in Northern Virginia. The pieces of the puzzle were coming together.

After the meeting, Fournier headed back to the Denver airport and then to San Diego. He felt deflated. All of the JTTF's work was down the drain. The reasons offered by the U.S. attorney didn't feel right.

"Did you and Click talk about it afterward?" I asked.

"Briefly," Fournier said.

"And what did you say?"

"We weren't happy. We would rather not say exactly what was said. There may have been some profanities in that"—Fournier paused, reliving the moment—"in that particular conversation."

It wasn't a big part of his investigation, because there was no connection to passport fraud, but in the course of his work Fournier came across at least two of the mug shots for the San Diego prostitution charges.

Our Fox team filed a Freedom of Information Act request with the State Department for Fournier's closed case file. There was no reason not to give us the file and redact the cleric's personal information. The State Department contact told Fox that its human resources department was now handling the matter. Things were not making sense. In the spring of 2010, the U.S. government placed the cleric on the CIA's kill or capture list, yet the State Department wanted al-Awlaki's permission to release the case file.

The search for the booking photos, the most compelling evidence that the cleric was a hypocrite, frustrated our investigation. The San Diego Police Department and the county sheriff were obvious sources for the mug shots. They told us the records were gone. A five-year rule called for the destruction of the records unless there was a criminal conviction.

Al-Awlaki reportedly got community service, a fine, mandatory HIV counseling, and three years' probation. Without a criminal prosecution, his indiscretions remained off the radar.

Why, I wondered, was the U.S. government holding on to information that could discredit the cleric among his followers and potential new recruits? We could get a mug shot of any celebrity, but not of a wanted terrorist? No question, a booking photo was powerful stuff. While senior U.S. government officials assured me that every tool in their arsenal was being used against al-Awlaki, they were sitting on the mug shots.

Federal Office Building
Near the Potomac River
March 29, 2010

"He's like the canary in the coal mine," producer Greg Johnson explains as we pile into a D.C. taxicab. Johnson is referring to former customs agent David Kane. Kane's firsthand account of al-Awlaki's reentry into the United States explains how the cleric slipped away.

An hour earlier, Johnson and I were sitting at a conference table in one of Washington's chrome and gray federal office buildings. The meeting followed lengthy e-mail communication about the project and why we needed Kane.

His government employer was asking us not to reveal his

current job or details of ongoing cases. The office where Kane works understood a basic fact that Fournier's State Department bosses apparently did not: the al-Awlaki case is closed. Details are in the public record. We will pursue the story with them or without them.

When we meet, Kane looks to be in his forties. A handsome man with a deep voice, he is very professional. He is matter-of-fact about the events leading up to and including al-Awlaki's reentry into the United States on October 10, 2002. He doesn't remember everything, but the picture is clear. Kane was following orders. Letting the cleric off the hook was not his call.

We later learn, through separate channels, that a political appointee at Attorney General Eric Holder's Justice Department was apparently putting pressure on Kane's office to nix our interview. The political appointee, a regular from the 2008 Democratic campaign, was worried that our story would make his boss look bad at a time when the attorney general was being roundly criticized for his indecision on prosecuting the 9/11 plotters.

Despite the pressure, Kane's shop held steady. The interview got the go-ahead. Johnson and I returned to Kane's office ten days later.

. . .

Former customs agent David Kane got his start in Baltimore in 1997 as a special agent assigned to the high-intensity drug-trafficking group. As Kane described it, he was tracking money laundering, narcotics, and smuggling.

He transferred at the end of 2001 to Northern Virginia,

where his responsibilities expanded. He tracked and choked the terrorist money trail. The project was known as "Operation Green Quest." Kane explained its work this way: "The mission . . . was to target the nodes of financing for terrorist groups and try to identify them and then dismantle them by criminal prosecutions and seizures."

It was a successful nationwide campaign. Connected to the American Muslim Council, Abdul Rahman al-Amoudi was prosecuted for illegal activities with Libya as well as immigration fraud. He was sentenced to twenty-three years in prison. According to Kane, a bizarre element of the case included a plot to assassinate the crown prince of Saudi Arabia.

This information got me thinking about the U.S. attorney in Colorado. Al-Amoudi was prosecuted for immigration fraud among other charges. Why was al-Awlaki a special case? Was he being protected? It was a hard idea to shake off.

After 9/11 Kane and his colleagues were running down a lot of leads with alleged ties to terrorism. Al-Awlaki's name was identified. Kane's group knew about his relationship to the hijackers. They were focused on the cleric who moved from San Diego to Virginia. "We were concerned about him because we realized he was residing in the Northern Virginia area leading up to 9/11 and he was the alleged spiritual adviser to [Nawaf al-Hazmi and Khalid al-Mihdhar] in San Diego.

"We wanted to see if he had a relationship with a certain group of individuals that we were investigating." Kane was deliberately vague. There was just enough detail to keep Greg and me interested.

"We focused on him. We were trying. We reviewed a lot of evidence. We conducted a lot of search warrants, based on that case. We did not find a link between that group and Awlaki."

"There was something about him or his situation that got your attention?" I asked.

"Absolutely," Kane replied without hesitation.

Kane said there were individuals who may not have had a direct role in a terrorist act, but who helped make it happen. They were spiritual advisers. They were facilitators. Kane and his fellow agents were worried. With his American citizenship, the cleric seemed untouchable.

In the summer of 2002, an agent at the FBI called in a favor. Pursuant to a separate investigation, not a customs case, Kane was asked to put a record for al-Awlaki in the Treasury Department's computer database.

With a little push, Kane filled in the blanks.

"What can you tell us about that record system or the database?" I inquired. "I think you're referring to the TECS system." TECS is an acronym for the Treasury Enforcement Communications System. It serves a lot of different purposes. In this case, it acted as a lookout. A subject record was created. The record was an insurance policy. With al-Awlaki's arrest warrant active, the feds wanted to know when he set foot in the United States.

Kane put it this way: "To make sure that he was, that if he came into the country, customs would identify him upon arrival . . . We would be notified, and the FBI would then be notified so they could have him arrested."

The timing was important. Was the "lookout" for al-Awlaki entered into the customs system about the same time the warrant was issued? Our team would learn that the timing matched and the same FBI agent was involved.

"So early in '02 or late in '02?"

"I'd have to say mid-2002 . . . somewhere thereabouts. I can't recall exactly."

"The FBI agent, Wade Ammerman, did he tell you why he wanted the record open?" I pushed Kane further. We both knew who the agent was—though now, for an unexplained reason, Kane chose not to identify the agent by name.

"The FBI had asked us to put the record in simply because they had a warrant for his arrest and they just wanted to make sure that upon arrival in the United States, they would be notified and he would be arrested."

Now the interview jumped forward to October 2002. Everything Kane told us was consistent with the customs logs first obtained by Sperry.

Early on the morning of October 10, the cleric and his family came into JFK, and Kane got an unexpected phone call or "notification" from the customs inspectors. "I, in turn, contacted the FBI to notify them that he was there and asked for further instructions to communicate to the inspectors. At that point, I was notified that the warrant had been rescinded."

Kane was matter-of-fact as he spoke. There was no emotion. I shouldn't have been surprised. It was not Kane's call. He was following the FBI agent's instructions.

"Did the FBI explain why the warrant was rescinded?"

"No, there was no explanation."

I came at the question another way. Confirmation that the FBI agent knew the status of the al-Awlaki warrant would be a critical detail in our investigation. "But the agent, Wade Ammerman, knew that it had been rescinded that morning?"

Once again, Kane avoided using the agent's name. "The FBI knew that it had been rescinded, yes. I don't know the date when [it] was rescinded, but he knew."

After the interview, I went back to the customs documents again. I pushed a stack of papers out of the way and laid the customs log out on the left-hand side of my computer. On the right-hand side, I placed the warrant.

There was something about the timing that bothered me—a lot. The customs log showed that al-Awlaki arrived in the early-morning hours of October 10, 2002. The notifications began at 0615. By 0740, Kane was told by the FBI agent that the warrant had been pulled.

But how would the agent know the status of the warrant unless he was working with the U.S. attorney in Colorado? Or, if he hadn't talked to the U.S. attorney, then the information had been relayed down the chain of command.

Suddenly it hit me: the timing was impossible. The court documents showed that the warrant was pulled on October 10, 2002—the same day al-Awlaki arrived at JFK. Given the two-hour time difference between eastern time and mountain time, it meant the warrant was still active at 0740.

This timing discrepancy meant the Justice Department's position would later fall apart.

I started doing the math. I did it several times. At 0740, it was only 0540 Colorado time. It meant the federal court was not open for business. It meant the warrant was still active.

Our team was dumbfounded. What was the FBI's motivation for allowing the cleric in?

Another discrepancy in the documents was about to become clear. One of our go-to resources was the 9/11 Commission Report. When we searched for the cleric, only a few references came up. There was a single footnote in the report about al-Awlaki.

Fox senior producer Cyd Upson was the one who put the final piece of the puzzle in place.

On her own initiative, Cyd searched the report. No matches were found for the agent's last name—Ammerman. It listed the agents by first name and the initial of their last name to protect their identity. The goal was to encourage agents to speak freely with investigators. Many were actively working cases.

When Cyd put in the name Wade, there was one hit, on page 517, footnote 33. It read "Wade A." It was the footnote about al-Awlaki. I got out my Palinesque reading glasses, and we combed through the small print.

On October 16, 2003, commission investigators interviewed Agent Ammerman. He had been described to me as a primary case agent for al-Awlaki. It was more than strange that a year after the cleric's mysterious return to the United States, Agent Ammerman apparently never mentioned the JFK episode or the arrest warrant to the 9/11 investigators.

The only reference to October 2002, when al-Awlaki mysteriously returned to the United States, was an FBI "EC," or Electronic Communication. ECs are intelligence reports, like internal memos, with a limited distribution. On October 8, 2002, the 9/11 Commission Report stated, an EC was written about al-Awlaki. It seemed related to his radical ties, but we could not be sure from the notation.

The timing made me feel sick. On October 8, Diplomatic Security agent Ray Fournier was told that the arrest warrant was being pulled by the U.S. attorney's office in Colorado. Also on October 8, an EC or FBI intelligence report was written about al-Awlaki.

The following day, October 9, the U.S. attorney's office in Colorado filed court papers to vacate the warrant. That same day, the cleric boarded a plane in Saudi Arabia for the United

States. On the morning of October 10, al-Awlaki was held for several hours and then ordered released by the FBI, even though the warrant was still active. It wasn't until later in the day that the arrest warrant for passport fraud was actually pulled in Denver. It was not until the following day, October 11, that the paperwork was filed by the clerk and became public record.

When I asked former FBI agent Brian Weidner for his take, he seemed to give a knowing smile. "Certainly a lot of coincidence there," he said.

"Are they coincidences, in your opinion," I asked, "or more than that?"

"The question really is, 'Was Awlaki flipped?'"

CIA headquarters
Langley, Virginia
October 13, 2010
1430 hours

"They are essentially traitors," twenty-nine-year-old John, a CIA counterterrorism analyst, said of the growing number of Americans buying into al Qaeda's cause. "They understand the West very well, and it's exactly what al Qaeda wants—they want Americans to do their dirty work." The whole topic disgusted him.

Earlier in this chapter, we met the hardworking career agents Fournier, Weidner, and Kane, who did the heavy lifting immediately before and after 9/11. Now there is a new generation of agents, analysts, and officers fighting al Qaeda in its various forms. I wanted to meet them. I wanted their assessment of the evolving threat.

Over a two-day period, I was given rare access to the new

generation of counterterrorism analysts at the CIA. I interviewed six who specialized in Yemen, Somalia, and North Africa, as well as Pakistan and Afghanistan. All of the analysts were under forty. I agreed not to use their real names or other identifying information in an effort to protect them and their families.

CIA analysts simply call it their "account." That's shorthand for their area of expertise and responsibility. With five years at the Agency, John's account was al Qaeda in the Arabian Peninsula—the same Yemeni group where the American cleric held court.

"It's been a growth industry, unfortunately, over the past several years." John was sitting directly across from me at the conference table.

The threat in Yemen, he said, was growing substantially. He said foreign fighters left Iraq and the conflict in Afghanistan and Pakistan because of increased U.S. counterpressure. A 2006 prison break, which critics of the Yemeni government claimed was an inside job, dumped the worst of the worst onto the streets.

"A lot of these guys were aides to Bin Laden. Fought by him. Were his mentees. Protégés of him. So they see the world through Bin Laden's eyes."

Twenty-eight-year-old Eleni was sitting on John's left, my right. From southern Illinois, she was high energy. During her six years at the Agency, she first covered Iraq and then moved on to Pakistan and now to Somalia.

Where the threat went, Eleni seemed to follow. Al Qaeda was more than the core group of Bin Laden and his deputies, like the Egyptian doctor Ayman al-Zawahiri. Eleni said people might be al Qaeda affiliated, al Qaeda aligned, al Qaeda inspired—the threats were simply multiplying. "They're not black-and-white, and they're overlapping and they're converging. And some people aren't fully committed but they can still blow up a bomb. . . . We're constantly finding new ones, unfortunately."

Twenty-seven-year-old Jean hailed from New Jersey. Her accounts included Pakistan and Afghanistan. The analyst's job was to understand why Americans and others would join a group dedicated to killing. In most cases, the dead were fellow Muslims. "They [recruits] don't feel included with their community and what they're doing. There's been talk about generational divides, that we're seeing more second-generation kids who are going to join the jihad."

Jean's observation caught my attention. It was close if not identical to those of former CIA official and Homeland Security intelligence chief Charlie Allen. Allen was the first member of the U.S. intelligence community to identify publicly the American cleric as a threat to U.S. national security.

Jean said the counterterrorism analysts were paid to understand how ideology, religious affinity, and other factors fueled the rage. "It's hard for us to relate to that but that is exactly what we are paid to do."

But as John pointed out, the pat explanations, like poverty and bad schooling, did not explain the whole picture. Al Qaeda was able to attract a diverse group with diverse backgrounds, including Americans. "It is not just the poor uneducated from sub-Saharan Africa. You've got a country like Haiti, one of the poorest countries in the world, and I can't name one al Qaeda operative from Haiti. So it's clearly not just a lot of the traditional factors that you hear in the media."

Thirty-six-year-old Joe was senior in the group. His portfolio included al Qaeda groups in southern Africa, al-Shabaab in eastern Africa, and al Qaeda in the Islamic Maghreb in northern Africa. When he first came to the agency in 2003, Joe worked al Qaeda senior leadership and its immediate circle.

Unlike John and some of the other counterterrorism analysts, Joe was not visibly angry or frustrated as he spoke about al Qaeda's new American recruits. He simply lamented the fact that Americans were now part of the equation.

Everyone in the group agreed that American and other Western recruits were the new gold standard. Al-Awlaki was the forerunner. The recruits blended in. Part of the attraction, according to Joe, was that Americans enjoyed more protections under the law because of their citizenship.

"These individuals have decided to place themselves within the ranks of al Qaeda and our enemies, and many are actually plotting attacks against the United States. And that's where the issue becomes very thorny."

Joe did not doubt their intentions. "They're very serious about what they are saying, and eventually they are going to kill people."

About 60 percent of the CIA's workforce joined the Agency after 9/11. While information about the demographic breakdown was not available, Agency officials said more officers than before joined with a second or even a third language. Being born outside the United States was an advantage. It was not an automatic disqualifier.

Joe began working terrorism issues in the mid-1990s. The FBI hired him after the Oklahoma City bombing. He left the Bureau in August 2001 for graduate school. When 9/11 happened, it drove him back to the mission; he joined the CIA in 2003.

"It was troubling. I was torn. In many ways, I felt that I had been working it all these years, and were there signs? Or was there something we missed domestically? That was a big concern of mine."

Thirty-two-year-old Sam was the only covert officer in the group. His intelligence career began with imagery analysis. On 9/11, he was working at a Navy installation on the Potomac River. "I was here in D.C. when that happened. . . . We could see the burning from the Pentagon." With the growing demand for counterterrorism specialists, Sam decided it was time to make the switch to the CIA and covert operations.

Thirty-three-year-old Susan came to intelligence right out of college. She also began her career in imagery analysis. For Susan, the 9/11 attacks were personal. It was one reason she'd stayed so long with intelligence work—eleven years. "September 11 really affected me at the time. I was working with a lady that I became very close with, and her husband was killed in the Pentagon."

There was a perceptible shift in the intelligence community's strategy after 9/11. In a separate briefing, a senior counterterrorism official agreed to discuss the overall threat picture on the condition that he not be identified by name.

The senior counterterrorism official said analysts were no longer desk jockeys. They were in the field more. They were in war zones. They were "forward deployed." "You have to go to areas where there's just no control. You are not out on the streets of Moscow," the senior counterterrorism official said. "You're in the tribal areas of Pakistan or you're in Mogadishu. You are just in a dangerous place. . . . That danger has gone up."

On average, the counterterrorism analysts now spent 15 to 20 percent of their time deployed. Joe, who covered al Qaeda senior leadership at the start of his CIA career, said the field time was invaluable. In 2003 or 2004, he deployed to South Asia. He would not be more specific. "It gave me a certain level of comfort and it gave me texture and clarity that I would not have had otherwise about the vastness of the area, the rugged terrain, the people. You can go into certain areas and see young kids carrying AK-47s."

Sam, the covert officer, said the forward deployments provided context. As far as sources were concerned, it helped analysts understand where the information was coming from. It helped them gauge whether a source was reliable. Could his or her intelligence be trusted?

He said there was no substitute for sitting in on a meeting with a foreign intelligence service. The CIA tried to leverage these relationships. "To be there, in the room, as those discussions are happening and not just get the readout that comes through the system. But [to] actually see the conversation and to know, by being in that room and asking that question right then, I got information that was vital to us evaluating this, determining what we are going to do."

And there was other intelligence to be picked up in the room. The body language of the foreign intelligence service officers could indicate whether they were open or closed to the CIA's requests. "If I hadn't been in the room the other people probably wouldn't have thought to ask that question."

Like tours in the military, these agents' deployments were becoming more frequent. The time away from base was being extended. In the last five years, John said, he had spent ten to eleven months on these temporary-duty assignments. "They are essentially war zone trips or tours," John explained. It was stressful for him and those close to him. "And the family gets antsy or they ask questions like 'Why do you have to keep going?'"

Eleni was single, though she spoke of a boyfriend at the Agency. Her family still lived in Illinois. Her dad carried around a printout from the CIA counterterrorism Web page. He proudly showed it to everyone who was interested in his daughter's career choice. "I wish I could tell them more, but I like that they have this vision of me as a female Jack Ryan."

She said the deployments were eye-opening, giving her a better understanding of the CIA offices or "stations" overseas and how they worked. The adrenaline, the rush of the mission, appealed to her. "I just spent three weeks in Africa with two days' notice and was able to pick up, hit the ground running, because it's the same job here that it is there. Work round the clock there, come back and publish a piece for the president the next day."

Eleni was petite, so her next statement was not surprising. "I had a rough time with Glock training, but other than that . . . that's where analysts are a teensy bit out of the comfort zone."

Susan was more practical. "What you learn on the trips, you bring back here and can give that much more. . . . It gives you a sense of the restrictions, the capabilities."

"And whether what you are asking is reasonable," I added.

Susan did not hesitate. "And if it's going to benefit the overall mission."

While the analysts spent more time in the field, back at headquarters in Langley, Virginia, the base of operations was also changing. The Office of Terrorism Analysis, or OTA, was the analytical arm of the Agency's counterterrorism center.

Eleni said the analysts were embedded with the "operators," or operations officers. Their offices and cubicles were together—not split up. "Historically the Agency was more stovepiped, where analysts would have one corridor and operational colleagues would have another corridor in the building, for example, and now we sit side by side."

As counterterrorism analysts, their main customer was the National Clandestine Service (NCS). They supported the NCS mission, which was to collect actionable human intelligence, or HUMINT.

"We're right there in real time getting that information." Joe said it was not unusual to watch a major terrorist pickup in progress. "We know that they're actually about to do some sort of operation overseas, an arrest, for example, or something like that. And that actually helps us enormously as we prepare our product for the next day to tell the president X, Y, and Z is happening."

There was no need to wait for the official written report. Joe and the other counterterrorism analysts incorporated what they witnessed into their write-ups.

Joe said success, like an arrest or disrupting a plot, was fleeting. If they celebrated, it was with doughnuts or a cake, and then reality set in. "The moment of happiness kind of goes very quickly. . . . Sometimes you've been following people for years. In many ways the real work begins once a person is picked up or once a plot is disrupted." Joe paused and then qualified his statement. They didn't always know whether a plot was disrupted or simply put off to another day.

The 2006 liquid explosive bomb plot began with a group of young British Muslim men, many of Pakistani descent, who planned to carry the substances onto jets in modified sports drink bottles, like those of Gatorade. Once onboard, they were to assemble the bombs and detonate them over the Atlantic. The plot was believed to be al Qaeda to the core. The men traveled from their base in Britain to Pakistan for recruitment and training.

Sam said the analysts knew the plot was serious but didn't have enough to know what the terrorists were up to. "There was a tremendous sense of relief when those arrests occurred, but there also comes with it a huge amount of trepidation because here you have operatives that are looking to employ a technique that the security measures at the time probably wouldn't have detected."

And there were lingering questions too. Were all of the terrorists and their associates in the net? "And how many other operatives were out there with the same sort of training, planning to carry out an attack?"

Al Qaeda's senior leadership, while diminished, was continuing to plan and attempt large-scale mass-casualty attacks. While the 2006 plot and the 2009 underwear bombing by al Qaeda in Yemen were disrupted, Joe said that another "surprise" could be imminent. "We were lucky. And sometimes, you know, luck is on your side. And we're happy that it didn't happen. But these are real and persistent threats that have come in pretty short succession, if you think about it, from 2006 and 2009."

"With the exception of Christmas, all the most dangerous plots to the homeland come from AQ core," the senior counterterrorism official said, reflecting on the reality of their work.

"Still?" I asked.

"Still," he answered. "They're the ones out there pushing."

Under the ground rules, the senior counterterrorism official had agreed to talk for thirty minutes. As we neared the end of the allotted time, he seemed to be enjoying the scope of our conversation. He stayed an extra ten minutes.

He said al Qaeda was clever. They were learning from their mistakes. "They've learned lessons about how plots have been broken up in the past and so they're moving in the direction of compartmenting more. Smaller cells. Looking for people who have natural access to areas."

Once the recruits had a few weeks or months of overseas training under their belts, with their clean backgrounds, they returned home to launch strikes. Faisal Shahzad was a good example.

Once back in the United States, the aspiring terrorist was frustrated, the senior counterterrorism official said. It was not surprising the car bomb fizzled. Shahzad's training by the Pakistani Taliban was inadequate. "He realized, 'I can't get some of this stuff here. Or the gasoline's different here, so how do I adapt this?'"

For terrorists who operated in the lawless border region with Afghanistan, known as the Federally Administered Tribal Areas (FATA), the training of foreign recruits went only so far. The senior counterterrorism official said the materials available to build a bomb in the wild lands of Pakistan were not the same materials found at American hardware stores.

The aspiring terrorist was at a loss. "And what you find [with] a lot of these guys [is], 'I have the instructions but I don't know what to do.'"

With the growing number of Americans seeking training or inspiration overseas, the senior counterterrorism official said the intelligence community was getting better at following them back and making the handover to the FBI. Continuity was important because some recruits might disappear overseas for five years, while the analysts might cycle through their assignments in a year or two.

In the case of Najibullah Zazi, who trained in Pakistan to attack the New York City subway system in 2009, the intelligence community knew he was out there, but when the pieces came together, not much time was left. "The window of time between when we found [identified] Zazi and when he was arrested was pretty short. We knew of Zazi as a concept for months. When we found him that window was short from the arrest and was shorter still between [the arrest and] when he was about to do something."

That experience weighed on the analysts as they tracked the threat picture in the fall of 2010. "A plot like this when we don't have all the insight into it. We are looking really, really hard."

Skill mattered, but luck would be on our side for only so long. The senior counterterrorism official said the American cleric Anwar al-Awlaki and others like him were aggressively encouraging followers to launch small-cell or lone-wolf attacks. They didn't want recruits to travel overseas for specialized training. "Their point is, 'Don't come here—you have what you need already where you are. It doesn't matter, strike a blow, do what they did at Fort Hood. Look at the impact this has, and all that I had here was a gun you could go to any store and buy.'"

Al-Awlaki's group, al Qaeda in the Arabian Peninsula, was different from the other affiliates, he said. "Two things set them apart. One is Awlaki and his reach. The other is that they've designed a bomb that can defeat basic airline security. Those two things give them cachet and give them influence."

And the group wanted to be a player on the world stage.

"Someone like Awlaki wants to be global. I think he sees himself more as a global, external operation, attack[ing] the West. Because that gets them attention, profile, money, recruits, etc. I think he subscribes to the al Qaeda thesis of the far enemy." The far enemy was the West and the United States.

While the al Qaeda core was surprisingly resilient nine years after September 11, the senior counterterrorism official questioned whether the affiliates like al-Shabaab in Somalia or al Qaeda in the Arabian Peninsula in Yemen could survive a major leadership shake-up.

The official compared al-Awlaki to the former leader of another well-known al Qaeda affiliate, al Qaeda in Iraq. The now dead leader of al Qaeda in Iraq, Abu Musab al-Zarqawi, was, like al-Awlaki, young and charismatic. In his propaganda videos, he was larger than life as he trained recruits. Right after U.S. forces killed al-Zarqawi in June of 2006, the official said, the number of attacks by al Qaeda in Iraq spiked, but two years later the group was diminished, and it never recovered. "Someone like Awlaki, there would be someone that would step in . . . but I think in some ways there is no one like him that we can tell out there."

Nine years without a mass-casualty attack on U.S. interests was weighing heavily on the al Qaeda core. Now, the senior counterterrorism official said, there was more blending of the groups like al Qaeda, the Taliban, and Lashkar-e-Taiba (LET), the group behind the commando-style attacks in Mumbai in 2008. The concept "the enemy of my enemy is my friend" was taking hold.

"If [al Qaeda] is going to get back—they have to do something that seems more spectacular," the senior counterterrorism official said.

"Are they still obsessed with planes? Mass transportation?" I asked.

"Both, both," he answered. "Or the Mumbai style—any terrorist looks at that and for two or three days that's all we saw on the TV."

And what about Bin Laden? While some U.S. officials argued that the predator drone campaign had him so far under a rock that he had become irrelevant, others questioned whether he was hiding in plain sight, perhaps near a major urban center.

"Do you still feel he [Bin Laden] is able to be in charge?" I prodded.

"Yeah. He's the one person that I think they look at. Given his role. He has a respect no one else does," the senior counterterrorism official responded. It was important to defeat the al Qaeda core in the FATA, and it was equally important, he said, to put pressure on the al Qaeda affiliates. The goal of the U.S. intelligence community was to keep the affiliates a regional problem that could be defeated with the help of local intelligence services.

In the fall of 2010, the threat picture seemed ominous. U.S. officials said there were multiple threat streams and multiple plots. They emanated from the tribal areas of Pakistan as well as from the affiliates in Yemen and North Africa. While they appeared to be directed at Europe, U.S. targets were not being ruled out. Even with arrests in France and the deaths of suspected German militants in Pakistan in October 2010, the threat was not diminished.

"Does it at all look like the pre-9/11 picture in your mind?"

The senior counterterrorism official paused to collect his thoughts. "It is worrisome. It is probably the most worried that

I've been in years, looking at it. Before 2006, with the airline plot, that was pretty clear something big was about to happen as well. This one is looking that way also. Something's up."

As of this writing, I don't know whether the plots were disrupted, were abandoned by the operatives, or were in some way successful. However, the senior counterterrorism official said there was a constant in their work. "The challenge is—there are things we know, things that we can do to increase our confidence, and things that we don't know."

Joe, the counterterrorism analyst who covered Africa, framed the challenge this way: "You're essentially looking through a soda straw at a conveyor belt of plotting that's going by. You see what you see. You don't know in what stage it's going by but you see several things go by. At some point a plot will fall off because the action arm decides they don't want to carry out the attack, or maybe it's been disrupted, or they run out of funding, or the people chicken out, you just never know. But rest assured there's something else coming down the line."

After two days of interviews, the CIA analysts had one final thought. They brought the conversation full circle to their predecessors, the CIA officers who worked counterterrorism before it was a buzzword. They worked the threat before it was the stuff of TV series and career fairs.

"It's not like, on 9/11, they left the building," Joe emphasized. "They're still down there, and many of them were our mentors and they taught us what to do and how to approach the issue. Our office wouldn't be what it is today had it not been for those people."

The covert officer Sam said their real dedication before 9/11 was somehow lost in the avalanche of criticism directed at the

CIA. "It wasn't for a lack of understanding the seriousness of the threat," Sam said. After the catastrophic loss, the pre-9/11 officers picked themselves up. They helped reorient the intelligence community to deal with the now-recognized threat. "For that reason, we certainly stand on their shoulders in many ways."

National Counterterrorism Center
Suburban Washington, D.C.
September 16, 2010
1300 hours

The display case is relatively small and, from a distance, unremarkable. Behind the heavy security, the memorial is powerful in its simplicity. It is a constant reminder of their mission. Inside the case, on the left is a twisted girder from the Twin Towers. On the right, there is limestone from the Pentagon. Behind both is a tattered American flag. By my count, thirty-two stars remain.

It sits in the lobby of the National Counterterrorism Center. It is not far from the main operations center, which is reminiscent of something out of a Hollywood thriller. The location is no accident. Hundreds of employees pass by the memorial every day.

Michael Leiter heads up the NCTC. He is grayer now than when I first met him as a senior deputy years ago. It's not surprising. The terrorists need to be right only once. The American people expect the NCTC to be right every time. As he conceded after the failed Christmas Day bombing, Leiter's own performance was under review.

Leiter says the memorial is a touchstone. When his employees are having a particularly bad day—enduring a lengthy or unproductive interview or getting annoyed by something or being delayed in traffic on the way to work—they should take a few moments and stop by to reflect on what the memorial contains and represents. If, after that reflection, they don't feel passion for the work, it's time to hang it up in the counterterrorism world. And that's okay.

"It's a way of bringing us back to the very, very real consequences of violent Islamic extremism in the world. That flag is torn and tattered but it's still there. We have to remember the people who died under rubble."

Leiter also sets a realistic expectation for the next generation of agents and analysts who are fighting this war. "We are a resilient country, and small attacks like that [Fort Hood, the failed bombings of Christmas Day and Times Square] don't threaten us, and the only way we can actually threaten our society is to overreact and give terrorists a victory that they otherwise wouldn't have."

• • •

After four months of negotiations, I was led down a nondescript hallway to an equally nondescript conference room to interview a group of analysts, most of whom worked in the NCTC's radicalization unit. They tried to walk in a terrorist's shoes, adopting the mind-set. They investigated why some Americans bought into the message of violent Islam and eventually went bad.

Five of the analysts were under thirty, and the old man in the group, at forty-three, was Joe. He was a contrarian by nature. As he spoke, I made a mental note not to confuse him with Joe at the CIA. I figured it was a popular cover name. "I hope you don't set up your book as, you know, the battle of the warriors." Joe held the room with his sarcastic tone. I knew Joe was deadly serious. He was tired of the stereotypes.

"He [the terrorist] wears a headdress and has a straggly beard and comes from far away. On the other side is a nice young man from the Midwest wearing a tie."

Joe came from a three-letter agency. I assumed it was the CIA or the NSA, though he would not identify it. His intelligence career began in 1989 with the Army, shifted to the FBI for five years, and now he was working the unit.

Joe continued his heavily embroidered narrative. "These two warriors, one with his noble Koran and his sword and the other with his newspaper and his Starbucks. Although they've never met, they are the most deadly enemies of all."

This group was not Jack or Chloe from the show *24*. No doubt they were bright and sharp, but if they didn't open their mouths, you would walk right by them in the mall. I imagined that was the point.

Each one brought a unique skill set. On my immediate left was Lisa. She was twenty-eight and married to someone in the intelligence community. She spoke softly and deliberately. Her background was in the FBI, based in the Midwest, handling sex offenders. Farther down the left-hand side of the conference table, beyond Joe, was Victoria. She was also extremely smart and extremely animated. She'd packed a lot into her twenty-four years. While at George Washington University, she had interviewed extremists in the United Kingdom via Skype. She worked for Homeland Security and Naval Intelligence before being detailed, or temporarily assigned, to the NCTC.

On the right-hand side of the table was Dawn. The twenty-seven-year-old and her family were from Pennsylvania. She was a Redskins fan even in the team's off years. Her background was also FBI. Next to Dawn was the nice young man from the Midwest with the Starbucks coffee Joe was poking fun at earlier. Jim was from just outside Pittsburgh. He was twenty-seven years old. Terrorist propaganda, like the al-Awlaki audio and video messages, was his specialty. On my right was Kevin. He was a twenty-six-year-old from Atlanta, Georgia. He was a civilian analyst for the Marine Corps before he formally joined the intelligence community. His focus was homegrown radicalization. He studied under one of the few radicals to have been successfully deprogrammed.

The NCTC was the most visible manifestation of the post-9/11 shift in fighting the war on terror. Staffed by more than five hundred people from the sixteen departments and intelligence agencies, the NCTC was "the primary organization in the United States Government for integrating and analyzing *all* intelligence pertaining to counterterrorism." Beyond preparing analysis and intelligence reports, it maintained the databases for the watch lists. The Terrorist Identities Datamart Environment (TIDE) was the broadest list, with about 500,000 entries. This information supported the Terrorist Screening Center and the watch-listing system.

If there was one phrase that made each one of the analysts cringe, it was "connecting the dots." Given their reaction, the wincing and the sighs, I immediately felt guilty for having used the phrase at least a thousand times.

After 9/11, the FBI was blamed for failing to connect the flight training, the hijackers, and the eventual plot.

Kevin was blunt. "Sometimes we don't know what the dots are and we have no idea which dots to connect. It is a very, very imperfect system and an imperfect world that we live in, where at times information is limited and lacking." Kevin put his frustration, and that of the other analysts, into words. "For me, connecting the dots, it doesn't mean much. I think it is trying to describe what it is we do without understanding what it is that we do."

Victoria said it was a cool phrase to throw around. As a culture, she said, we were too reactive and too busy playing catchup. "The really crucial thing for our organization is trying to get ahead of these trends," Victoria said earnestly. "And I think that's what 'connecting the dots' means. It's thinking ahead and it's trying to understand the terrorists from their perspective, not just ours."

To get ahead of the trend, analysts like Kevin track the terrorist messages on the Web and in open-source intelligence. The analyst wanted to understand the terrorists' mind-set. "I look at very strategic issues, terrorist intentions, the big grand picture of where is this all going? Where is this whole issue that we are focusing on going to be in ten years, twenty years down the line, because for them it seems it's not a generational issue, it's a forever issue."

Kevin's explanation was a kick in the gut. Terrorists didn't operate on a four-year election cycle. Theirs was a struggle that lasted for generations.

Kevin emphasized that the target was always moving. "It's a constantly evolving issue we're trying to understand and we are trying to really grasp, so we can figure out where we're going to have to put our focus in the future."

Though I was sure he would hate the comparison, Kevin was a human sponge, out there every day, absorbing the radicals' messages and picking up their signals. He consumed all the clues they left in plain sight. The propaganda, and the way a cleric like al-Awlaki or a spokesman like Omar Hammami saw himself, told the analysts a lot about the movement and its future direction.

Kevin emphasized that having studied at the knee of a former radical Islamist gave him an advantage. It was an experience most pre-9/11 agents never had. "Having the opportunity to learn from someone who actually subscribed to the ideology, it was very eye-opening."

Kevin implied that the message was insidious. "It can seem very innocuous, it can seem very innocent at the time."

He said there was not a one-size-fits-all formula for predicting who was vulnerable to radicalization. "There is a confluence of factors and it's not always a one moment, one time, tipping of the level. It can be a long process for these individuals to believe these things." There was no single trigger, Kevin said. "It's not always social. It's not always religious. It's not always cultural. It's sometimes . . . all three or sometimes it's two, it's sometimes one, sometimes none."

Lisa chimed in. She said extremists isolate themselves from mainstream society. She also agreed with Kevin that their motivations vary. Some of the best indicators of their future intentions were on the Web, in their chat rooms. "It's no longer a matter of them . . . having to travel overseas. They can reach out to these people online, and that is a real problem."

Lisa said there was a revolution under way on the Web. It was first noted, she said, by the NEFA Foundation, the same group that discovered al-Awlaki's statement praising the alleged Fort Hood shooter, Major Nidal Hasan, as a hero. Lisa said al Qaeda leadership was now harnessing technology to build support. "Al Qaeda leaders have even referenced some of their soldiers by their monikers, online monikers." Lisa laughed nervously as she gave one example: "So, 'Hamza1998, hey, shout out to him for doing what he did.' That is something we would never have seen before."

Lisa said this development was important. The al Qaeda leader and his online followers had never met in person. They had no direct personal contact. And now an al Qaeda leader was giving a shout-out based on what was written in a Web chat room.

Dawn's focus was also open-source collection and analysis. She said blaming the Internet was simplistic, even ridiculous. "[After] 9/11, when we were trying to grasp . . . what [was] causing people to do things, there was at least a wave of 'the Internet made people do things.' The Internet is an inanimate object. The Internet can't make people do things."

Dawn said she followed the basics: the messages, the audiences. The extremists used the Internet as a tool to send out their "bad ideas into the world."

It was hard to draw conclusions about an entire workforce from six people. But it was clear that they brought different experiences to the table. According to a spokesman for the NCTC, about two-thirds of the workforce joined the intelligence community after 9/11. While no specific data could be provided on the NCTC staff's average age or their foreign-language skills, I was told that members of the radicalization unit were typical.

Joe said a lot of agencies and the FBI threw around the word "diversity" but didn't really mean it. But at the NCTC, diversity helped them pinpoint the threat. "Here I think actually diversity is what gives us understanding. If we have people who have never broken the law, we can't understand lawbreakers. If we have people who are not of a certain religious or cultural background, we will not have truly intuitive understanding."

Self-confessed architect of 9/11, Khalid Sheikh Mohammed, in an undated photo. *NEFA Foundation*

Sketch from Khalid Sheikh Mohammed's arraignment, June 2008. When asked to review the sketch by the U.S. military prior to its release, KSM said the nose was wrong and ordered the sketch artist to fix it. *Janet Hamlin*

Accused 9/11 conspirator Ammar al-Baluchi (also known as Ali Abdul Aziz Ali) in an undated photo. He is a nephew of Khalid Sheikh Mohammed. *NEFA Foundation*

Accused 9/11 conspirator
Walid bin Attash in an undated
photo. His family and Osama
bin Laden's family were friends.
Memri.org

New Mexico–born cleric Anwar al-Awlaki in a
recent al Qaeda propaganda video. Al-Awlaki is
the first American on the CIA's kill or capture
list. *Memri.org*

Daphne, Alabama,
native Omar Hammami
in a high school picture.
NEFA Foundation

Omar Hammami leading fighters
from al-Shabaab (al Qaeda's
affiliate in Somalia) against
Ethiopian troops. The video
surfaced in 2009. *NEFA Foundation*

Omar Hammami in a 2010 propaganda video, in which he asks fellow Muslims to support the orphans of al-Shabaab fighters in Somalia. The golden symbol in the lower right means the video was made by al Qaeda's media production branch.
Memri.org

Faisal Shahzad, seen here in a propaganda video, pled guilty to driving a car bomb into New York's Times Square in May 2010. The Pakistani Taliban trained Shahzad in the failed plot.
Associated Press

Major Nidal Hasan is accused of the Fort Hood massacre. This camera phone image was taken after his first court appearance at Fort Hood in June 2010.

In this photo, released by the NYC police department, Colorado resident Najibullah Zazi is extradited to New York, where he faced terrorism charges. Zazi and others plotted and failed to blow up the New York subway system in September 2009. *Associated Press*

Raised in South Florida, Adnan Shukrijumah is one of the FBI's most wanted terrorists. Shukrijumah, who has become chief of the terror network's global operations, allegedly trained Zazi for the New York subway attack in the tribal areas of Pakistan. *Associated Press*

Former diplomatic security agent Ray Fournier (far right) on assignment in Belgium, spring 2000. Less than eighteen months later, he began the Anwar al-Awlaki investigation for the San Diego JTTF. *Ray Fournier*

Former Customs agent David Kane tracked and convicted terrorists after 9/11, including Anwar al-Awlaki. *Terence Golden*

Lt. Col. Tony Shaffer in Kabul, Afghanistan, 2003. Shaffer is a thirty-year veteran of the Army Reserves. *Anthony Shaffer*

Edward MacMahon Jr., one of the nation's leading national security defense attorneys, represented Ali al-Timimi, who is serving a life sentence for inciting jihad against the United States. Al-Awlaki mysteriously showed up at al-Timimi's home in October 2002 with a government witness. *Edward MacMahon Jr.*

John Galligan (left) is the defense attorney for Major Nidal Hasan. Hasan and al-Awlaki exchanged at least eighteen e-mails before the Fort Hood shooting. Galligan accuses the Defense Department of withholding evidence. *Associated Press*

Mohdar Abdullah was held as a material witness after 9/11 because of his close ties to hijackers Nawaf al-Hazmi and Khalid al-Mihdhar. Along with the hijackers, Abdullah also worshipped at al-Awlaki's San Diego mosque. © *Ernie Grafton/San Diego Union-Tribune*

Carlos Bledsoe, seen here in his high school graduation portrait, is now accused of opening fire on a military recruitment center in Little Rock, Arkansas, in 2009. His father, Melvin, says everything changed for Carlos after he was allegedly radicalized at a mosque in Nashville, Tennessee. *Melvin Bledsoe*

Nawaf al-Hazmi (left) and Khalid al-Mihdhar (center and right) met on a regular basis with al-Awlaki at the San Diego mosque. The American cleric is described as the hijackers' spiritual adviser. *NEFA Foundation*

Pilot Hani Hanjour took over Flight 77 along with al-Hazmi and al-Mihdhar. Hanjour was also connected to al-Awlaki through the cleric's mosque in Falls Church, Virginia. *NEFA Foundation*

Charlie Allen, whose career spanned fifty years in the U.S. intelligence community, was the first government official to publicly identify Anwar al-Awlaki as a threat to U.S. national security. *Associated Press*

Former CIA and NSA director General Michael Hayden. *Associated Press*

Major General Dale Meyerrose of the Harris Corporation. Meyerrose is a former chief information officer for the Office of the Director of National Intelligence. *Harris Cyber Integrated Solutions*

San Diego police arrested Anwar al-Awlaki twice for soliciting prostitutes. This mugshot is from 1997. *Federal Bureau of Investigation*

I made a few quick notes. Even the mere suggestion of criminals working counterterrorism made the discussion more interesting.

No one at the conference table wanted to predict the future, but Anwar al-Awlaki was certainly in the picture. Lisa said his power was obvious. He was one of us. "He is an English-speaking individual. He is very charismatic. He can really talk about his experiences in America because he's lived in America. He kind of bridges the gap. . . . He really understands the culture."

After college in Colorado and further study in San Diego and Washington, D.C., al-Awlaki polished his sales pitch. "He gives good arguments, rational arguments. It is a perceived rational argument. They are perceived as rational, the way he gives them."

Lisa predicted that the problem was not going away anytime soon. "If we could give you an exact prototype of [the next terrorist] that would go out and do this, we would already have finished this problem and be done. We'd be out of a job."

Victoria predicted that there would be a lot of threats outside of al Qaeda, and it would be tough to prioritize where the counterterrorism analysts' attention should go. "We all chase the new shiny object. There are going to be a lot of shiny objects. . . . There's a lot of people that are converting, that come from all sorts [of backgrounds], and this isn't about Islam per se, the mass-movement frame."

All of the analysts were close to the work. I found their criticism of the unrelenting focus on al Qaeda especially noteworthy. Joe said that Iran was probably a more serious threat and more worthy of the U.S. government's attention. "Terrorism . . . is more than al Qaeda, and I think that's been lost, which

I think is a shame. It's very upsetting when you see a young person potentially radicalized to attack the United States, but there are tens of thousands of people at a rally burning American symbols.

"The phrase 'state-sponsored terrorism,' I mean Iran, I believe to be more powerful than al Qaeda. . . . I don't know what the pie chart might look like in terms of analytic effort or budget or anything of that stuff or news coverage or any of these other things, but I think if the pie chart were somehow looked at, whatever the metric is, that al Qaeda is bigger than it ought to be."

I brought the conversation back to a simple question: Why was it that 9/11 inspired some young Americans to serve their country, while it inspired others to destroy it?

As with the day JFK was shot, or Princess Diana died in a Paris tunnel, everyone in the room remembered where he or she was when the attack unfolded.

Jim, who said passion was the skill he brought to the table, changed career paths after 9/11. The transition was gradual. He abandoned corporate law and developed an interest in international affairs. Some of his professors, who had worked intelligence before entering academia, were influential. They planted the seed. "When 9/11 happened I didn't have an immediate reaction to it and change career patterns," Jim explained. "But it sort of began the walk down the path to greatest interest in international affairs."

Dawn said the scar on the Pentagon changed everything for her. "That is an image that is still in my mind every day when I come to work. . . . I felt I needed to do something more actively effecting change."

Dawn slowly and deliberately described that morning in northern Virginia. No cell phones worked. There was no communication. She could not reach her family in Pennsylvania, where one of the planes went down. As she spoke, my mind was pulled back to Ground Zero.

I don't talk about it much, but I was in New York. I spent several weeks reporting from the site. There was one woman whose name I can't remember, but whose story I won't forget.

She was middle-aged, ordinary-looking, slightly disheveled. She was scraping ash from the roofs of abandoned cars into a shoebox as she walked toward our live reporting position, near the site of Building 7, which collapsed after the Twin Towers.

I stopped her and asked what she was doing. In a flat voice she told me that she was from Chicago, and that on the day of the attacks, she got in her car and started driving. She drove all day and all night. Her sister had been at a breakfast meeting at Windows on the World, the restaurant at the top of the World Trade Center. She knew that her sister was dead, and that she would never find her body. She said she needed something to take home and bury. The ashes from the abandoned cars, in a shoebox, would do.

When Dawn mentioned her grandfather's stories about Pearl Harbor, it suddenly jolted me back into the discussion. She said his recollections of America under attack in 1941 struck a chord with her sixty years later. "I don't want to say it was the same event, but it was interesting how emotionally it had a big impact on him and his generation I think in the same way it did on ours. . . . It brought [the threat] home and now you needed to do something about it."

Dawn could not explain why Omar Hammami reacted so

differently to 9/11. Hammami was raised a Southern Baptist by his mother. His father was an immigrant from Syria. Dawn believed the conflict at home and the search for an identity shaped his view of 9/11.

Maybe it was true, but I didn't feel that "finding yourself" was a good excuse for Hammami and others. Who grows up without conflict in their home? Who reaches their late teens and doesn't have questions about their identity? Prosecutors felt there was no excuse for the path Hammami chose. In August 2010, the feds unsealed charges against fourteen people for allegedly supporting and in some cases funding al-Shabaab. Hammami was among them.

The analysts easily put their finger on the most significant change in intelligence work since 9/11. If the pre-9/11 generation of agents and analysts were accused of stovepiping information, the next generation claimed it was committed to sharing it. That was not to say the endeavor was easy going. But some of the changes were as simple as forcing the agencies and bureaus to share an office like they did at the NCTC. "This community is a community that is full of closed doors with little peepholes. It's not famous for opening doors to other people," Joe explained. "You put three agencies in the same building and they have to stumble across each other on the line for coffee anyhow."

Joe said that something more profound than sharing a break was going on. "9/11 was not the date that it changed, but sometime in the past decade what happened was that the way to win was not to keep your secret to yourself. . . . Now, I don't think there's this jump-ball mentality. I think there's now more of a team mentality. The doors are still closed and locked and there are still various separations we have, for good reasons. . . . I think I have seen a cultural shift. And I don't think it is necessarily attributable to a generational shift."

Dawn posited that the sheer volume of information coming in, between eight thousand and ten thousand reports daily to the NCTC, made sharing data a matter of survival. "When you see that piece of information, the onus is on you as the analyst to know who your analytic counterparts are and reach out to them, analyst to analyst. Either pick up the phone or walk across the building or send an e-mail."

Whether from goodwill, the importance of the mission, or necessity, Dawn said, the counterterrorism community was less territorial. "There is so much work to go around, I think there is very little 'This is my lane, I need to write on this.' We do a lot of collaborative products, a lot of work that involves multiple agencies and offices."

Success for the group was defined by preventing attacks. But they all recognized that most of their successes or failures would not be understood for years to come. It was like working in a vacuum.

"I think it's scary in a way," Victoria said. "You may see immediate successes and get the kudos now but in reality a lot of times we see five years later the impact of these immediate decisions and how they did lead to failures." Countermessaging— designing and propagating a different narrative to discredit the extremist ideology—was a work in progress. "We're not going to know for five, ten years what our effectiveness is. Especially with trying to understand radicalization and countermessaging. There's not an immediate impact that's readily measurable."

After two hours in the conference room, the problem boiled down to this: al Qaeda was no longer a vertically integrated company where the CEO called the shots. It was diffuse and diverse. It was a movement. It was a set of ideas. We were in the middle of something larger. Victoria said we didn't understand the implications yet.

"We're already seeing al Qaeda has changed. We're not fighting the same al Qaeda that we were on 9/11. I don't even think this entire enterprise really understands what al Qaeda means to begin with. What is al Qaeda?"

And when they were wrong, when there was failure, their mistakes were played out in a public way.

"We're in a profession that we see our failures in the newspaper and people who don't know what we do are very capable of claiming that we've made obvious errors." Joe leaned forward onto the table. "Since they don't know what we know and we don't necessarily have an opportunity to speak for ourselves, we just, so to speak, have to take it."

Critics of the NCTC said it was another layer of bureaucracy that made the problem worse. Now there were a lot more fingers to point blame when things went bad. But in those chaotic days after the attacks, Joe said with a touch of sarcasm, the buck always stopped with the FBI. "My perception, the feeling after 9/11, was that everybody blamed the FBI. . . . You could circle it with a big red pen. And every other agency was trying to blame every other agency, and the FBI was there to blame."

Mr. Smith's of Georgetown
Washington, D.C.
October 11, 2010
2015 hours

It would be wrong to shut the FBI out of the conversation. So I tracked down Daniel L., a forty-five-year-old FBI counterterrorism agent. We had met eighteen months earlier because of our shared interest in Anwar al-Awlaki. We sometimes have drinks in Georgetown. Out of habit, he always sits facing the doorway. With a career spanning the pre- and post-9/11 periods, Daniel provides context on the FBI blame game.

Daniel insists that the young agents are an asset, but there is no substitute for experience in the field and on the street. "In the age of push-button gratification, many younger agents are inclined (because they've learned) to sit behind their computer and make cases and win battles 'one click at a time.' This is dangerous," Daniel cautions. "Winning battles will always require 'boots on the ground,' human intelligence, and generally getting dirty and face-to-face."

Because of his deep Christian beliefs, Daniel is not afraid to discuss the darkness of radical Islam. "The enemy is a mix of thug and wicked ideologue. Many today will not use the term 'wicked' because of its abuse in the movies and overuse with regard to 'the opposition.' I believe, though, that it is rightly applied to the radical, Islamic jihadist that the Obama administration is so desperate to assimilate, ignore, or redefine."

Daniel speaks at least three languages. From time to time he pocket calls me and I can hear Arabic or Spanish in the background. I like Daniel a lot. He is impossibly handsome in the way most people imagine an agent should be. But the longer we have known each other, the more I have come to respect his relationship with the mission.

"I am one of the most critical people I know of. Most FBI agents are. But when the Bureau is wrongly accused, it's demoralizing and infuriating. . . . The soapbox expert is one of the dumbest, most illiterate, most ignorant, most hateful people I know."

Daniel is certain that mistakes and missed opportunities cannot be eliminated. Intelligence, like humans, is imperfect. He is smiling as our conversation ends. There must be another plane to catch. "Even as the terror groups abound and self-propagate, their failure is sure, determined by the destructiveness and violence of their message."

· ·

CHAPTER 4

JUSTICE DELAYED

Fort Hood, Texas

June 1, 2010

0827 hours

I am watching the clock. Court is due to begin at any moment. It's already hot at Fort Hood. A sprawling base of nearly 335 square miles, it is larger than most American cities.

Earlier that morning, our crew drove through the security gate. More than two dozen checkpoints line the base perimeter. Fort Hood is home to one out of every ten active-duty soldiers in the U.S. Army. After an ID check and a quick scan of the rear seat, we were told to proceed and to "have a great day!" Everyone seemed happy in a Wal-Mart greeting way.

More than a hundred reporters are here—print, radio, local TV, and CNN. The three national broadcast networks are noticeable by their absence. By contrast, it was wall-to-wall coverage in November 2009, less than a week after the shooting, when President Obama spent four hours on the ground at the memorial service. Now, as the wheels of justice grind slowly onward, interest at the networks has apparently waned.

This morning, a problem is on the horizon. With only ten guaranteed seats for reporters in the courtroom, most of us will be left in the press center, a large temporary workspace with a closed-circuit television feed of the proceedings. I know from my experience at Guantánamo that there is no substitute for being in court just a few feet from the defendant. The only story worth telling that day will be a firsthand account of events inside the Lawrence H. Williams Judicial Center.

The night before, we met briefly with Hasan's lawyer, John Galligan. His office is on the main strip near the base. Galligan is hard-charging and direct. He talks and walks a mile a minute. His matter-of-fact manner is laced with frustration. It comes through most when he talks about his client's seven gunshot wounds and his pretrial confinement. Hasan is being held at the county jail—not at a hospital.

Hasan is paralyzed from the upper chest down. He will be shackled on his way to court. With disdain, Galligan says it is Army procedure.

With persistence and a little charm, our producer, Gretchen Gailey, secures a seat inside. We arrive a few minutes early. The courtroom is surprisingly small. There are a handful of rows, each with about fifteen seats.

I try one seat, second row, on the far left. It is right behind the defense table. Before long, I abandon the seat. I'm worried it will be too close and I will see only the back of Hasan's head. His face and his expressions will be the narrative. Will Hasan show any emotion? Or will he be cool and detached, knowing his fate seems certain?

Now I try the right-hand side of the courtroom, in the second row. If Hasan comes through the front left door next to the bench, as we all expect, I will have a good profile shot. I am banking on the fact that his lawyers won't block my view.

This morning, I am feeling nervous. It's not a feeling I am used to. I'm uncomfortable as well. Hasan faces thirteen counts of murder and thirty-two counts of attempted murder. Today's hearing marks the start of a long process. Hasan will face an Article 32 hearing. It is the military equivalent of a civilian grand jury. Witnesses will be questioned. The investigating officer will decide if there is sufficient evidence for the case to go forward. It sounds very clinical. In this case, a military court will ultimately decide whether a soldier who is paralyzed should now be put to death.

I change seats one last time. Now I am in the second row, left side of the court, on the aisle seat. I figure I'll be able to see Hasan fairly well, and I'll be able to see the prosecution at the same time.

Just before 0830, I hear the courtroom's back door swing open. I look over my right shoulder and see a man dressed in his Army fatigues. He is a major. He is sitting in a wheelchair, and under his own power he is making his way to the defense table. His legs are thin and limp as they lie in the vinyl seat.

I am less than fifteen feet away when I make eye contact with Major Hasan. His eyes are clear and determined. Then he turns away from me as he directs his attention and all of his physical energy to pushing the wheelchair forward two feet, then another two feet.

This moment sets the tone for the hearing, which lasts about an hour. Throughout, Hasan answers the investigating officer clearly and directly, or he indicates that he has no questions. Periodically, his body slides down in the wheelchair, and he uses his hands to raise himself up.

There is only one moment when I feel that Hasan, who wraps himself in a blanket because he complains of chills, disconnects from the proceedings. He stares into space and rubs the side of his face with the blanket as the defense and prosecution teams discuss the FBI's handling of the ballistics report inside the Readiness Center. It is the closest the hearing comes to reliving the events of November 5, 2009.

As court finishes, Hasan is wheeled out the back door. From my seat, I can see what appears to be a holding area. I lean forward because my sight line is not good. Much of the activity is blocked, but it appears the soldiers guarding Hasan are putting shackles on his paralyzed legs.

This time, when I catch Hasan's gaze, I do not see cool determination. In an instant, I see a flash of darkness. Maybe it's the pain. Maybe it's regret or lingering anger. Maybe I'm reading too much into his stare.

The timing is uncomfortable too. It is the Tuesday after the Memorial Day weekend. While the country is honoring its war dead, Hasan's attorney is complaining that the Defense Department is holding back key evidence.

In a classic document dump, before the long weekend, two thousand pages of evidence were unloaded on Galligan. After months of delay, the Defense Department's strategy was simple. There would be no time for Hasan's modest team to review the new material and to prepare for Tuesday.

But there is one thing Galligan can tell me. He still doesn't have all the e-mails exchanged by Hasan and the cleric, Anwar al-Awlaki. A former intelligence officer who is now studying the insider threat says there are at least eighteen including al-Awlaki's responses.

While the attorney charged with defending a man's life can get only nine e-mails, a congressional committee manages to get all of them after threatening to subpoena Defense Secretary Robert Gates and Attorney General Eric Holder.

"What is so special about these e-mails?" I mutter under my breath.

Maybe my federal law-enforcement contact is right; maybe the e-mails are innocuous. But I am not one to see ghosts where there aren't any. There is something about the e-mail traffic that is dangerous for the government.

. . .

"Catherine, you've done that story a thousand f—— times!" I never thought I would hear a Justice Department official use the f-bomb while discussing the 9/11 families. "They are just whiners," the official explained. I think, though I cannot be sure, that the official added "f—— whiners" to punctuate our conversation.

The story of a seventy-two-year-old retired school nurse named Mary Novotny prompted the f-bomb. Her son Brian worked on the 104th floor of the north tower. When American

Airlines Flight 11, piloted by Mohammed Atta, slammed into the World Trade Center, there was no way down. Smoke and flames choked the three stairwells from the 92nd floor up. Mary said her son's phone records showed he was on his cell until the moment the tower collapsed at 1028.

It was a sad image that would stay with me. In my mind's eye, I could see her poring over phone records, looking at the time stamps. She needed to understand her baby's final minutes.

In May 2009, this retired school nurse turned activist wrote to President Obama. She attached a picture of her son. "I never got a response to my letter; I don't know if he saw it, so I plan to write again," Mary said hopefully.

In the fall of 2009, Novotny made the journey to Guantánamo. It was a tribute of sorts. "I promised Brian, I would be in the courtroom for these trials if we ever got justice. I would be there as his witness." Novotny paused and composed herself. "Just to sit in the courtroom was good for me to do."

Nine months earlier, with the stroke of a pen, President Obama seemed ready to fulfill an oft-repeated campaign pledge. In January 2009, he promised to close the detention camps at Guantánamo Bay. According to a former senior Bush administration official, the top White House lawyer, Greg Craig, was advised not to set a deadline, but team Obama could not resist.

The sweeping gesture would uproot the lives of many 9/11 families, including Novotny's. Closing the camps within a year was the administration's new slogan. The concept was neat and tidy. It would later be seen as arrogant and naive.

Those who bothered to brief themselves fully on the issue should have known that the plan would fail until two questions were answered: How will you find a home for the Yemenis who make up half of the detainee population? And how will you prosecute some of the most hated men in America's history?

The administration promised to include the 9/11 families in its review of the Guantánamo cases. It sounded good. Most of all, it was consistent with candidate Obama's stated goal of transparency. Like so many campaign promises, it was harder to keep once in office.

Novotny's story was the second time I'd profiled a 9/11 family. Earlier in the summer of 2009, I reported on Melissa and Brian Long. Like Mary, they secured a seat in the Guantánamo court as part of a Defense Department lottery for the 9/11 families.

The Longs were so angry about the administration's handling of the families and the Guantánamo review that they could not be silent any longer. It was their first television interview. Melissa's feelings boiled just beneath the surface. "I didn't go in there [a meeting with administration officials about the Guantánamo review] prepared for how frustrated I'd be afterward," Melissa told us on their backyard deck in suburban Washington.

Melissa lost her boyfriend, a New York City firefighter, on 9/11. Brian's parents were both on Flight 77. It slammed into the Pentagon at 0937. The couple met through Brian's aunt.

There is raw video footage of Melissa's boyfriend as he walked with his team toward the Twin Towers. Within an hour of that video being filmed, he and his buddies would be dead—crushed by the massive weight of the buildings.

"It's hard to watch, but I knew he was doing what he wanted

to be doing." Melissa paused as she reflected on the videotape. Her voice was strong. "He was a really proud fireman. He loved his job, and there are not many of us that can say we love our job as much as most firemen do."

On that crisp and clear September morning, Brian was in Leesburg, Virginia, on jury duty. His parents were flying, but he didn't know what plane they were on. Brian's brother went to their parents' home to confirm: Flight 77 was on their itinerary.

Both Brian and Melissa said they were disappointed, even disgusted, with the new administration and what was billed as a meeting. "They listened: only one of them took notes," Melissa explained. "And the rest of them took flak. They took a lot of heat. There were a lot of questions unanswered."

The captain of the USS *Cole*, Commander Kirk Lippold, was also at the family meetings. I met him for an interview in Lafayette Square, the park behind the White House.

"I believe there was a predetermined agenda by this administration," Lippold snarled. "The meeting with the families was nothing more than a farce."

While military commissions were far from ideal, the commander, Mary, and the Longs said they backed them. Even then, six months before the attorney general announced a proposed venue for the trials, the 9/11 families suspected he was leaning toward criminal prosecutions.

"I believe that they based it on a court-martial system, and if it is fair enough for our own military, why is it not fair enough for these war criminals?" Melissa asked. "And what if the cases get thrown out? Are we going to let them go? How would any of us feel if they just walked away from that? I know that I would personally be devastated."

Gordon Haberman was also on the Longs' trip to the Navy

base. After we connected on the phone, he sent me a picture of his daughter Andrea. She was also killed at the World Trade Center. I moved Andrea's picture from Gordon's e-mail to the desktop on my computer. I would open it periodically.

Andrea's smile was remarkable. She was showing off an engagement ring. I imagined it was how her father wanted the world to remember her. After 9/11, the same picture was used for posters and T-shirts in her family's search through lower Manhattan.

Haberman seemed frustrated too. But on his trip to Guantánamo, he went out of his way to visit the 189th Military Police Company. Gordon wanted to thank them for their service.

Gordon's picture was on the JTFGTMO Web site. Gordon was shaking hands with a soldier who looked to be in his early twenties and grasping the soldier's arm with his left hand. The two were smiling at each other. The connection was powerful. "I thought we should meet them to thank them ourselves," Gordon told the military reporter. "They're the ones who deal with the [detainees] every day. We can go home at night and forget about them."

Novotny's story and those of the 9/11 families who traveled to the military hearings struck a nerve. I was eager to hear the Justice Department's side of the story, but I was starting to wonder if there really was one.

The Justice Department official boasted that there were lots of families who thought the administration's Guantánamo review was going well. When I asked for their names so that I could contact them directly, I was told that the department was protecting their privacy. When I asked if the department was willing to give the families my contact information, I was told it was not possible at the time.

Instead, a Justice Department spokesman provided a written statement: "The task forces welcome this input [a reference to Mary, Melissa, and Brian]. . . . Capturing a wide variety of views on issues related to detention policy and Guantánamo Bay will only help the task forces make more informed decisions and recommendations."

By the fall of 2009, Holder's Justice Department and the Defense Department were under pressure. After the president promised to close the detention camps, the military commission hearings were put on hold pending review. Every few months, the administration had to ask the military judges for more time before the trials resumed. In mid-September, the top Defense Department lawyer promised a decision in sixty days.

Just one month later, in October 2009, President Obama endorsed military commissions. It was a system that candidate Obama had not favored. Yet now in the Oval Office, Mr. Obama saw a role for the military hearings.

The White House talking points touted the new and improved commissions as a fair and impartial process. The implication was that the Bush team had designed a system where justice was not possible.

President Obama's Military Commissions Act of 2009 was virtually identical to President Bush's Act of 2006, except for some minor changes that codified existing practices. For example, evidence of statements obtained through torture or coercion could not be used.

The ACLU's Jameel Jaffer, a leading expert on the commissions, said there was a serious credibility problem. The commissions, he said, were a second-rate system of justice because the act failed "to bring the tribunals in line with the Constitution and the Geneva Conventions."

Despite the groundwork laid by the administration to curry public favor, Friday, November 13, 2009, would prove to be a cursed day. Early that morning, we were notified that the attorney general would be holding a press conference. Given the importance of the announcement, one detail surprised me. The president would not be there to back up Eric Holder. Mr. Obama was traveling overseas. I would later conclude that the White House desired some distance from Holder in case the 9/11 decisions went south.

Before he made his decision public, Holder said the choice he faced was monumental:

> I've only been Attorney General for eight or nine months, and I think this is about the toughest decision that I've had to make as Attorney General; trying to balance the need to ensure that we maximize our chances of success and hold accountable the people who committed these heinous offenses, while at the same time adhering to what I think has been a guide for this administration, adherence to the rule of law.

The federal court in the Southern District of New York got the nod. The five 9/11 suspects, including Khalid Sheikh Mohammed, would be transferred to a prison near Ground Zero. Two teams of prosecutors were tasked with the trial. One team came from the Southern District of New York, and the other team came from the Eastern District of Virginia. Both offices had lobbied hard for the case. It was a career-making opportunity.

The transfer meant that the 9/11 conspirators, who were from Pakistan, Yemen, and Saudi Arabia, were entitled to the same constitutional rights as U.S. citizens. They would enjoy the presumption of innocence. If acquitted, the men stood to be released.

"I would not have authorized the prosecution of these cases unless I was confident that our outcome would be a successful one," Holder told the packed news conference. In addition, five detainees would have their cases heard in the military commissions.

An important detail was absent. Holder did not explain where the military trials would happen: Guantánamo or a new secure facility in the United States?

Right out of the gate, Commander Lippold questioned why military commissions were good enough for some detainees and not for others. "If the military commissions process works and the administration believes that it can try terrorists under that venue, then why not try all of them?"

Detainees like Abd al-Rahim al-Nashiri, linked to the USS *Cole* attack, Abu Zubaydah, an alleged operations chief, and Khalid Sheikh Mohammed were special cases. U.S. officials said the three men were waterboarded in secret prisons overseas. For each of the men, the CIA program would become a trial within a trial. Holder and others knew it. That is why the attorney general hinted that the 9/11 suspects could be prosecuted without evidence from the Agency's program. "I will say that I have access to information that has not been publicly released that gives me great confidence that we will be successful in the prosecution of these cases in federal court."

But Holder's predecessor, Michael Mukasey, was critical of the decision. Mukasey's opinion had punch. He was the judge in the first World Trade Center trial. "I can't see anything good coming out of this. I certainly can't see anything good coming out of this very quickly, and I think it would have been far preferable to try these cases in the venue that Congress created for trying them and where they were about to be tried."

In other words, why did the Obama administration even bother to work with Congress to revamp the military commissions if they weren't going to be used for 9/11 cases?

Knowing what was coming down the pike, Senator Lindsey Graham, one of the few Republicans who supported closing Guantánamo's detention camps, spoke to me a week earlier. In the interview, held at his office in the Russell Building, steps from the Capitol, Graham was blunt. "And let me just say the president, quite frankly, has screwed this up," he said. "You know, he announces on the first day of his being inaugurated that he's going to close Guantánamo Bay, and he didn't do the hard stuff. And I've been talking with him for months about this—you gotta think this thing through."

I sat there silently.

"I think there's a war within the White House about what to do. I have tried to be an ally on closing Guantánamo Bay. . . . I want to hear the secretary of defense tell the nation he believes the mastermind of 9/11 should go to federal civilian court and be given the same constitutional rights as any common criminal, any American citizen."

On November 13, 2009, Graham's office was silent. One of the senator's aides told me that the White House asked him not to comment further until he met personally with President Obama.

It was not all doom and gloom around Washington. Others were effusive in their praise. In a statement, the ACLU said the decision to try the men in federal court "is a huge victory for restoring due process and the rule of law, as well as repairing America's international standing, an essential part of ensuring our national security."

And the president, who was traveling in Asia, gave a brief statement: "I am absolutely convinced that Khalid Sheikh Mohammed will be subject to the most exacting demands of justice. The American people will insist on it and my administration will insist on it."

Fridays are notorious in Washington for dumping bad news. And this Friday the thirteenth was no exception. On the same day the 9/11 venue was announced, Greg Craig, the White House lawyer who had steered the Guantánamo review and the closure of the camps, resigned. There was no immediate explanation. The net effect, and probably the desired effect by the White House, was to bury Craig's departure and the 9/11 announcement on a Friday when the president was out of town.

One question hung in the air. Was Craig the scapegoat for the president's imploding plans to close Guantánamo by January 2010? The deadline was only two months away.

The timing of these announcements allowed Mr. Obama to distance himself from the decisions. But before it was over, the president and the country's top law enforcement officer would muddy the waters even further.

Holder's announcement was part of a steady stream of events. It was designed to bolster the administration's position that the 9/11 suspects should be treated as common criminals. But each carefully choreographed event seemed to backfire, or at least to provide a new opportunity for critics.

Less than a week after the Justice Department news conference, federal officials from the Bureau of Prisons and the Defense Department embarked on a very visible and highly publicized tour of a potential detention site. The prison in Thomson, Illinois, was the frontrunner. About 120 miles west of Chicago, it was in the president's home state. Though it would have to be bought from the state and renovated at an estimated cost of $172 million, it was the administration's preferred choice. While supporters championed the creation of thousands of new jobs in a town of less than six hundred, some Illinois Republicans were already saying no to Gitmo North.

"We're not in the business of giving constitutional rights to terrorists, " Representative Donald Manzullo said. "That's the reason that Guantánamo Bay was set up in the first place."

"I could say we've become the laughingstock of the nation because of our corruption," Representative Judy Biggert explained. "Now, we're going to be the dumping ground for dangerous criminals. And why? Because we need money?"

Outside observers, including Cully Stimson of the Heritage Foundation, a valuable contact who was the top policy adviser for Defense Department detainees under the Bush administration, was critical of the White House and its meek approaches. "They didn't even begin to view any prisons in person until well after the summer. Which shows me that they were gun shy to get out and roll up their sleeves and do the hard work they need to do."

Former New York mayor Rudy Giuliani put it this way to *Fox News Sunday:* "It would seem to me what the Obama administration is telling us—loud and clear—is that both in substance and reality, the war on terror from their point of view is over. We're no longer going to treat people as if this was an act of war."

And soon the president and his attorney general would be undercutting the very system they sought to showcase for the world.

After the 9/11 announcement, Congress weighed in with multiple hearings on the Hill. One session began with a friendly question by a senior Democrat on the Senate Judiciary Committee. Senator Dianne Feinstein of California wanted to know whether there was enough "clean" evidence to convict the men. "I assume that the reason you made the decision is because you believe that there is sufficient untainted evidence to obtain a conviction. Is that correct?"

"That is correct," Holder said.

In an interview with NBC News, the president sounded equally confident. Prosecuting Khalid Sheikh Mohammed would be a slam dunk. "I don't think it [the venue choice] will be offensive at all when he's convicted and when the death penalty is applied to him," the president insisted.

Mr. Holder's and the president's statements seemed benign. But their logic was jacked up. They opened the door to the legitimate criticism that their statements would taint the jury pool in New York City, and anywhere else in the nation. "The defense will file a pretrial motion before the judge and say, 'Your Honor, we respectfully move to dismiss the charges,'" the Heritage Foundation's Cully Stimson said. "The president himself and the attorney general, the top law enforcement officer in the United States, have guaranteed conviction. What juror is not going to want to at least fulfill the president's and the attorney general's desire?"

Privately, some government lawyers on the military commissions bristled. One military officer told me that a U.S. attorney could be fired for making such prejudicial pretrial statements.

Perhaps this was why, in the same interview with NBC, the president, who was a Harvard-trained lawyer, suddenly backed off the slam-dunk-conviction claim. "What I said was people will not be offended if that's the outcome. I'm not prejudging. I'm not going to be in that courtroom. That's the job of prosecutors, the judge, and the jury."

On Capitol Hill, the fallout from a potential acquittal raised other questions.

"Are you concerned that a judge may say you've made an election, an election to try these terrorists as a criminal . . . you cannot go back and revert to the laws of war. . . . Are you worried about that?" Texas senator John Cornyn asked Holder.

"You cannot, perhaps, indefinitely detain somebody but you certainly can detain somebody for lawful reasons." Holder's statement was designed to calm fears that the 9/11 suspects could be freed on a technicality. But, there was a problem. The administration could not showcase the "fairness" of the U.S. justice system while at the same time, for political reasons, assuring the public that a conviction was a done deal.

Was terrorism a war to be fought on a global battlefield, or were al Qaeda and its followers the equivalent of a massive criminal problem? The administration's logic for sending some cases to criminal court and others to military hearings did not clarify matters. If anything, the fuzzy logic used by the White House, and by extension by the Justice Department, to make these decisions showed that there was no guiding legal principle.

The attorney general dropped the cases into two neat legal baskets. Alleged terrorists who hit civilian targets were sent to federal court. Those who attacked military targets were sent to the military commissions. Simple. Done.

Just a week after the announcement, the Senate Judiciary

Committee put Holder's logic to the test. "Isn't it true that on 9/11 the United States Pentagon, the center of the defense establishment, was directly attacked by the people who had declared war upon us?" Republican senator Jeff Sessions asked.

"Yes, there's no question that is true. One of the factors— it's one of the factors that I considered in making this determination. The number of people who were killed on 9/11 were largely civilians," Holder responded. The trap was being laid.

On the USS *Cole* attack, Holder stuck to the same reasoning. "An attack on an American warship, it seems to me, is something that is uniquely situated for a military commission as opposed to an Article III court."

The top Republican in the Senate, Mitch McConnell, ramped up the pressure. "Is the administration not telling terrorists that if they target defenseless U.S. civilians on our own soil they will get the rights and privileges of American citizens?"

McConnell's question gave everyone pause. The administration was not making a meaningful legal distinction in the cases. From a public-opinion standpoint, the administration's stance was a loser all the way. With a little more digging, another case underscored the administration's troublesome position.

I knew this obscure case from my trips to Cuba. Noor Uthman Muhammed was accused of running an Afghan training camp. It was called the Khalden Camp, and by all accounts, it was an extremely social place. Shoe bomber Richard Reid said he remembered al Qaeda conspirator Zacarias Moussaoui from the camp. At least two of the 9/11 hijackers were graduates.

Let's assume Muhammed, charged with running the camp, trained terrorists to attack civilian targets. Following Holder's logic, Muhammed was a candidate for federal court. He trained men whose sole purpose was to murder the average American. But with great fanfare, Holder claimed Muhammed's case was one of five earmarked for military trials.

Asked about the inconsistencies, a Justice Department official offered a strained explanation that the decision was part of a "careful, exhaustive, legal and factual review." It looked good on paper: professional and to the point. But when you parsed the words, it didn't mean much.

By December 2009, a grand jury was seated in New York City. An indictment was expected shortly—in a week or two at most. The plan was to pull the military charges once a federal criminal indictment was secured. But weeks passed and nothing was announced. The delay apparently forced the hand of military lawyers in an unexpected way.

Military lawyers wanted to preserve their legal position in case the 9/11 trials came back to them. As a result, the charges filed in 2008 were withdrawn without prejudice, which meant that military charges could be brought again in the future. Now, eight years after the murder of nearly three thousand Americans, no one was charged with the crime.

I printed out the charge sheets. Years of hard work were dispensed with in the crudest of ways. A thin black slash was drawn across each of the 104 pages, and above the slash were initials and the date "21 Jan 10." I put my head down on my desk. I felt physically sick.

• • •

While the administration defended its decision, the system and the American people were tested. No one within the intelligence community or federal law enforcement publicly predicted the use of an underwear bomb. But John Brennan, the White House homeland security and counterterrorism adviser, should have known better. The Saudis had briefed Brennan after the kingdom's counterterrorism minister was injured in a nearly identical attack.

Umar Farouk Abdulmutallab was a young Nigerian who came from a wealthy family. I knew his family's London address from my time working for ABC News on Carburton Street in the city's West End. The Nigerian student and his family lived a stone's throw from the old ABC bureau. It was just north of Oxford Circus and a few blocks from Regent's Park.

In those days, the ABC London bureau was the hub for foreign news. With a half dozen correspondents, including Pierre Salinger, President Kennedy's former press secretary, there was no better training ground for a young reporter. With my boss in Saudi Arabia during the first Gulf War, I was left in charge of radio.

One day, I smelled smoke. Were the circuit boards outside our compact radio studio overheating? Naturally, I searched for the source. As I poked my head around the doorway, toward Pierre's office, the smell got stronger. And when I mustered the courage to look inside his office, I saw Mr. Salinger at his desk.

His grin was a mile wide. His black leather gentlemen's boots were up on his desk. He was smoking his trademark cigar. In one hand he held a lighter. In the other hand, he held a bunch of papers. Flames leaped from the bottom corner of the sheaf. "Don't mind me," he said with a smile. "I'm just burning some documents." I managed a lame response like "Okay then. No problem. Let me know if you need anything else."

My early training at ABC News London taught me how to navigate unusual circumstances and personalities. It taught me never to ignore a lead—even the most bizarre. This training came in handy when a pair of explosive-laden underpants became the focus of federal investigators at the highest level of the U.S. government.

The White House was quick to defend its decision to read the Nigerian suspect his rights. Under the law, the FBI can stall. It is known as the "public safety exception." If there is an imminent threat to the public, agents can question a suspect without the Miranda warning.

On December 25, 2009, no one knew if the Nigerian was acting alone or if other underwear bombers were in the air. After just fifty minutes of questioning, the twenty-three-year-old lawyered up and shut up. On the Sunday talk shows, then White House spokesman Robert Gibbs claimed the impossible. "FBI interrogators believe they got valuable intelligence and were able to get all that they could get out of him."

The claim contradicted statements of current and former FBI agents. Based on the pictures I'd seen, Abdulmutallab's crotch was so badly burned that the pigmentation appeared to be gone. He was probably screaming and incoherent. The agents were not eliciting information to specific questions. They were more like stenographers.

A former FBI counterterrorism negotiator, Chris Voss, who maintained his contacts in the Bureau, backed up my hunch. "The description that's been relayed to me makes it hard to believe that he was making much sense at all. He was burned very badly in a very private area. That amount of intense pain is going to disrupt anybody's thought processes."

Voss said that it takes multiple contacts with a suspect to build a rapport. It was possible, he said, to turn a proven terrorist into an intelligence asset who can be a window onto future attacks. "Once they've told you everything they possibly can, they're probably in a position to give you [a] good assessment of what people might do and what plans might be formulated."

There was no question in my mind that valuable information was lost. "Actionable intelligence" referred to information good enough to do something with—such as the identities of other recruits, the locations of training camps, the name of the bomb maker.

The attempt on Flight 253 initially sounded like a crude operation. But two days into our reporting, we knew that the plan was well executed. A former head of the Transportation Security Administration told me that the Nigerian's seat, 19A, was an automatic red flag. It was over the wing and the fuel tank, and terrorists knew this section was the structural equivalent of the aircraft's Achilles' heel. If the device had detonated, the fuel tanks could have accelerated the explosion, increasing the likelihood of blowing a hole in the skin of the plane and destabilizing the wing.

The timing of the attack was curious, and still is. We don't know why the young Nigerian waited so long to detonate the device. The reason may come out during his trial or in a plea agreement. But by waiting until the plane's descent, Abdulmutallab lost an important advantage.

A hole in the skin of an aircraft is more serious at a high altitude, above ten thousand feet, where the speed and the air pressure are more likely to cause structural failures.

Steven Emerson of the Investigative Project provided the following analysis: "They had the right explosive to cause maximum damage. They were actually using human mules essentially as the delivery device."

No one was consulted in advance about the decision to read Abdulmutallab his rights. The powerful admission of this fact came in testimony before the Senate Homeland Security Committee three weeks after the failed attack. Neither the nation's top intelligence official, the director of national intelligence, nor one of his senior deputies, nor the secretary of Homeland Security was asked on Christmas Day whether the Nigerian student should be Mirandized.

Senator John McCain posed the question at the Senate hearing: "I understand, Admiral Blair, in response to Senator Collins [Republican of Maine], you were not consulted as to what venue the Christmas Bomber would be tried in. Is that correct?"

Director of National Intelligence Admiral Dennis Blair: "That's correct, yes sir."

And then McCain worked his way down the witness table.

"How about you Mr. Leiter?" Michael Leiter was the head of the National Counterterrorism Center.

"No, I wasn't," Leiter responded.

Then Senator McCain turned to Janet Napolitano, the secretary of Homeland Security.

"No."

In a separate hearing on the Hill, FBI director Robert Mueller confirmed that he was not in the loop either.

"Were you contacted about whether or not this individual should be treated as an unlawful enemy combatant or a civilian criminal?" Senator Jeff Sessions asked.

"No," Mueller answered before defending his agents. "In this particular case, in fast-moving events decisions were made appropriately. I believe very appropriately, given the situation."

And Defense Secretary Robert Gates was in the dark too, according to his spokesman, Geoff Morrell.

"So he was never consulted on reading his Miranda rights?" a reporter asked.

Morrell: "I don't believe so, no."

So who exactly made the call? At least five senior administration officials, including the nation's intelligence chief, were not consulted about the decision. To be clear: Abdulmutallab was not a shoplifter. It was not a minor case. He tried to kill 278 passengers and 11 crew on Flight 253 as well as innocent people on the ground.

When pressed, a Justice Department spokesperson would not say who authorized the decision or how high up it went. In addition, a new group expressly created by the Obama administration to handle high-value interrogations was not in play either. ("High-value" was the term applied to Khalid Sheikh Mohammed and others like him.)

The High-Value Detainee Interrogation Group (HIG) was announced with much fanfare after the CIA's terrorist-interrogation program was abolished. The formation of the HIG was another sweeping gesture to show that the Bush era was over. Interrogators were limited to the tactics of the Army Field Manual. Critics argued that the manual's protocols were less aggressive than the day-to-day methods used by big-city detectives.

When Abdulmutallab got on his flight, four months after the HIG was supposed to be set up, the unit was not operational. In other words, the HIG was not called in because it didn't exist.

Blair sounded discouraged and defeated as he addressed the committee. "We should have automatically deployed the HIG; we will now. We'll make a new mistake. We won't make that one."

Even the White House spokesman couldn't shoot straight. A month after the failed bombing on Flight 253, court documents showed that Abdulmutallab was charged in a Detroit court on December 26, the day after the attempt. Asked when the president was told that the suspect would be charged, White House press secretary Robert Gibbs made an impossible claim on *Fox News Sunday:* "The charges didn't happen until several days later."

In the midst of the chaos and incriminations, former CIA director Michael Hayden wrote a lengthy piece about the case in the *Washington Post.* Hayden left no doubt that intelligence about al Qaeda in Yemen and its immediate plans was lost for good. Hayden argued that Abdulmutallab was not "an isolated extremist" but the "tip of the spear of a complex al-Qaeda plot" to murder U.S. citizens.

There was only so much bashing the Obama administration could take. By February 2010, White House counterterrorism adviser John Brennan was on the offensive. "I'm tiring of politicians using national security issues such as terrorism as a political football," Brennan said on one of the Sunday talk shows. "They're going out there. They're unknowing of the facts and they're making charges and allegations that are not anchored in reality."

Brennan claimed that the Republican leadership in the

Senate and the House as well as the ranking Republicans on the Intelligence committees were briefed immediately. He claimed the lawmakers were told that Abdulmutallab was in FBI custody. Then Brennan seemed to stick the knife in and twist it. "They knew that an FBI custody means that there's a process that you follow as far as Mirandizing and presenting him in front of the magistrate. None of those individuals raised any concerns with me at that point. They didn't say, 'Is he going into military custody? Is he going to be Mirandized?'"

The response from Republicans was fierce. In a statement, the Senate minority leader Mitch McConnell said that Brennan was "clearly trying to shift the focus away . . . from their [the administration's] bad decisions." The ranking Republican on Senate Intelligence, Kit Bond of Missouri, disputed the claim. "Brennan never told me of any plans to Mirandize the Christmas Day bomber."

A spokesman for the House minority leader John Boehner described the call as "short" with little detail. And the ranking Republican on House Intelligence, Pete Hoekstra of Michigan, said Brennan was flat-out wrong. "His credibility now has been blown. He's gone out and he's questioned the integrity of leading members of Congress. And we all have the same memory of what happened that night."

At the height of the Abdulmutallab fallout, Mayor Michael Bloomberg pulled the plug on the 9/11 trials in New York City. The mayor's sudden reluctance was significant. He offered the obvious reasons: the trials would be too expensive and too inconvenient. The trial put a giant bull's-eye on millions of people and the financial center of the U.S. economy. Everyone knew New York City was already a target.

Now the White House had to step in. The president and

others were "reviewing" Attorney General Eric Holder's call to send the 9/11 suspects to downtown Manhattan. The president had distanced himself from Holder's original decision in November. Now he could step in and do damage control.

Pittsburgh Children's Hospital
February 24, 2010
1240 hours

Our younger son, Peter, is lying on the gurney. The recovery room is a familiar place to us. As a baby, Peter nearly died from a rare form of liver disease. With no donor available from the national waiting list, I gave 20 percent of my liver to help Peter.

The transplant was a miraculous surgery, but I always feel that our four-year-old is living on borrowed time. He should be dead, but with prayer, the help of our family, and medical advances, he is alive—and right now, he is very mad at his mother.

As a favor to the nurses and the technicians, I held him down when the anesthesia took effect for a liver biopsy. Every time I look in Peter's eyes, I feel that working mother's guilt. It is so hard to leave him and his brother, Jamie, behind, especially when I go to Guantánamo.

In the recovery room with J.D., I am holding my Black-Berry. One message has my attention. It is hard to ignore. It is from one of the 9/11 lawyers, who says the Defense Department is now blocking visits with their clients.

My lawyer friend sends me proof that the Defense Department is meddling again with the Guantánamo cases. The e-mail from the office of the staff judge advocate for high value detainees (HVDs) clearly states that the Defense Department's top lawyer must okay all meetings between the defense attorneys and the 9/11 suspects. Only written requests will be considered: "Your legal meetings . . . will not proceed without approval of the DoD General Counsel. . . . the request should explain . . . the need for such a meeting in light of the fact that the commissions case has been dismissed without prejudice."

My contact says the defense attorneys' e-mails are going unanswered, which is why he wants my help. I am told on the phone by a Defense Department spokesperson that there is no change in policy. The lawyers are not being blocked.

"Are you sure that is your position?" I ask the spokesperson on the other end of the phone. I hate shooting the messenger, but sometimes it's necessary. I suspect the spokesperson is passing on the line fed by superiors.

I am direct. After Peter's liver transplant when he was five months old, my reporting changed. Once you face the prospect of your child dying, there is a new fearlessness to your work. Nothing will faze you. "I have seen the e-mail traffic. I want to be sure the Defense Department's position is that there is no block on the lawyers' visits."

Peter rests quietly in the gurney. J.D. is losing patience because I am now on the phone—doing a live report—for the Fox News Channel, from the recovery room.

We won't have the final liver biopsy results for a week, but after an initial screening, we are told that Peter's liver cells look healthy. There is no sign of rejection as his doctors feared.

At 1313, less than an hour after my live report on the phone, another e-mail drops into my box. It is from my lawyer friend. The block has been lifted. No explanation is given: "JTF-GTMO has been directed by the department to facilitate scheduled legal meetings with your clients for this week. . . . please contact me if you would like to either 1) request that the meeting time be extended today; or 2) request a meeting for tomorrow before your flight."

"Goddamn them," I say to myself. I don't like the bad behavior of bureaucrats. The relationship between a lawyer and a client, even if the client is an alleged terrorist, is supposed to be sacrosanct.

. . .

By the spring of 2010 everything was on hold, from closing Guantánamo to the criminal and military trials. Released in May, a damning and long-awaited Senate Intelligence report seemed to rub salt in the wounds. Staffers on the Senate Select Committee on Intelligence concluded that there were "systemic failures across the Intelligence Community" that led to the attempted Christmas Day bombing. It said that the NCTC, the center created after 9/11 for analyzing and integrating all intelligence possessed by the U.S. government, failed in its mission. If the failure of 9/11 was caused by not connecting the dots, the failure of the attempted Christmas Day bombing was caused by not taking ownership of the information.

In defense of the NCTC, the amount of data coming in was mind-blowing. No solid figures were available until Michael Leiter, head of the NCTC, spoke up and vigorously defended his organization.

Leiter's defense came at the Aspen Security Forum. Admiral Mike Mullen, chairman of the Joint Chiefs of Staff; Husain Haqqani, the Pakistani ambassador to the United States; and

Michael Chertoff, the former secretary of Homeland Security were among the featured speakers.

Leiter claimed that a series of errors prevented Abdulmutallab's name from making the no-fly list. And even if all the dots had been connected, Leiter claimed, that would not have been enough. The bar was set too high. While not getting into specifics, citing classified information, Leiter said the threshold was now lower.

At least ten thousand people in the U.S. government had access to the intelligence that Abdulmutallab was a known or suspected terrorist. Among them were analysts at the National Security Agency, the State Department, and the CIA.

As for the volume of information, Leiter finally put a number on it. Between eight thousand and ten thousand reports came into the NCTC daily, including at least forty threats and distinct plots. This excluded threats in Iraq and Afghanistan.

The Senate Intelligence report did not finger a single agency or bureau or individual for failure. There was more than enough blame to go around.

Abdulmutallab's father had warned the CIA officer at the U.S. embassy in Nigeria that his son was an extremist. A memo or cable was written, yet the State Department officer in another part of the embassy did not revoke the young man's visa.

Worst of all, analysts had underestimated the threat posed by al Qaeda in Yemen. Analysts believed the group was only interested in launching attacks within Yemen rather than in the U.S. homeland, even though, six months earlier, the group had launched an attack in neighboring Saudi Arabia.

The same month that the Senate committee slammed the

U.S. intelligence community over the underwear bomber, the system was tested again.

My first tip on the car bomb in Times Square came at the White House Correspondents' Dinner. It is an annual event— often referred to as the "prom"—for journalists, politicians, and movie stars who long to rub elbows. The venue sounded glamorous—the so-called Reagan Hilton, where the fortieth president was shot.

The event, while fun, was a little overrated. It felt like Black Friday at the Mall of America. Getting a drink was a major accomplishment. Talking over the din was not worth the effort.

As dinner was signaled and everyone shuffled toward the ballroom, I saw James Gordon Meek, a reporter for the *New York Daily News*. We both covered national security issues, so we ran into each other a lot. We had bonded when we sat across from each other on a C-130 flight to Guantánamo for Khalid Sheikh Mohammed's arraignment in 2008. I am relatively short at five feet four inches. James is a mountain of a man—at least six foot seven.

Even in his tuxedo, James was on the story. As we passed each other, he leaned over and said something. I couldn't hear him, so he crouched down and spoke directly into my ear: "Terror Pixie"—my friends used this nickname a lot—"just a heads-up, something is going down in Times Square. Police Commissioner Ray Kelly and Mayor Bloomberg just took off out of here!"

A lot of threads were coming together. The American cleric, Anwar al-Awlaki, was connected to the shooting at Fort Hood. We knew he exchanged e-mails with the alleged shooter, Major

Nidal Hasan. Al-Awlaki was also connected to the attempted bombing on Christmas Day. We confirmed that he was the middleman who hooked up Abdulmutallab with the bomb maker. And now in May 2010, Faisal Shahzad, a naturalized U.S. citizen and "fan" of al-Awlaki's online lectures and CDs, drove a car bomb into Times Square.

Guantánamo Bay, Cuba
Latitude: 19 degrees 54 minutes north
Longitude: 75 degrees 9 minutes west
July 6, 2010

Two days after the nation celebrated its independence, we arrive at Guantánamo Bay for another round of President Obama's military commissions. While the hearings are held publicly, there is virtually no coverage in the mainstream media. That must be how the administration wants it, I think. Out of sight and out of mind.

As I walk down the mobile staircase, the sun is already high in the sky. It is hot and humid. At the McCalla Hangar, we are assembled for the security brief. New rules are in place. There is an edge to the discussion. Four of our colleagues with the major newspapers are now banned because they published information already in the public domain.

We are told a mysterious tale about a journalist who made a detailed sketch of the high-security courtroom. It was confiscated by the military because the sketch included the entry and exit points and overhead cameras. The briefer makes it sound like the reporter was working for terrorists. When I ask for more information, my question is directed to the Pentagon.

We are reminded that Guantánamo is a military facility and that under all circumstances clothing must be worn to the communal showers. We later find out that a pregnant representative from a nongovernmental organization set alarm bells ringing when she walked to the showers with only a towel.

And finally, Glass Beach is closed. Or at least, we can no longer access the beach from Tent City, where reporters are housed. The beach is where journalists go to swim, or drink, or hook up, depending on the time of day. "I know the answer," our Russian cameraman, Grigory Khananayev, says in his heavy but charming accent. "Now, the military, they are afraid that the al Qaeda men will wear scuba suits and come up along the beach and attack us."

It is sundown as we eat at one of the picnic tables. We are enjoying one of Guantánamo's most popular meals—jerk chicken from a restaurant called the Jerk House. We order the usual sides of rice, beans, and corn on the cob.

Grigory is right. Paranoia is settling over the camps and the court. It is no surprise. The groundwork was laid a year earlier.

. . .

In June of 2009, six months after President Obama announced he would close Guantánamo within a year, things weren't going well. Only a fraction of the detainees had been off-loaded to friendly nations.

One group was problematic—the Uighurs. They were Chinese Muslims who were picked up in Afghanistan after 9/11—many of them around Tora Bora, where Osama bin Laden famously slipped through the grasp of coalition forces.

The men were ultimately cleared for release by the military, but they could not be sent home. All sides in the Guantánamo debate agreed that the Chinese would torture or kill the Uighurs. But no country was brave enough to step forward and take them, because they feared retaliation by China.

I pressed the Pentagon spokesman, Commander J. D. Gordon, for a tour of Detention Camps 4, 5, and 6 and of Camp Iguana. The first three camps ranged from minimum to maximum security. Iguana was different. Nestled on the cliffs behind wire fences were modest bungalows. It was home to the Uighurs. Rumor had it that Pizza Hut delivered there.

Commander Gordon was reasonable. He made it happen. It was a decision many up and down the chain of command would ultimately regret. At the camp, an extraordinary scene unfolded. The Uighurs staged a demonstration.

They held up their government-issued art pads like placards. One of the Uighurs turned the pages. The protest was inflammatory and clearly aimed at President Obama. They compared the United States to "Double Hetler [sic]" and even attacked the commander in chief. One asked in English, "Is Obama a communist or a democrat?" They accused the U.S. government of oppressing them like the Chinese.

The accusations really stung. My husband would later comment, "The Uighurs lived in China. Believe me, they probably know a communist when they see one."

Multiple sources told Fox that the Uighur incident was highly embarrassing for both the White House and the Defense Department. Already on a short leash, reporters were reined in further. The beat reporters, who routinely covered the military commissions, were affected most. Defense Department press officers said we could no longer cover the hearings and the detention camps on the same trip. They said it wasn't a change in policy but a change in practice. If we wanted to tour the camps, we had to leave and make a second trip to the island, with a stop in Florida.

Meeting the Defense Department's requirement would be time-consuming and expensive. The department knew that media companies faced big budget cuts. There was no way to justify a second trip because the military refused to drive reporters fifteen minutes across the base.

It was a shameful and arrogant effort to reduce media coverage. As one military source told me, the goal was to "get a lid on the situation." And it did.

Bryan Whitman, who carried the title of principal deputy assistant secretary of defense for public affairs, wrote in an e-mail that touring the camps was not possible on the trip even though the court schedule allowed for it: "The time period and trip you reference is for Military Commission motions."

In another e-mail, Geoff Morrell, Defense Secretary Gates's spokesman, questioned why reporters wanted to see the camps more than once: "Haven't you visited the detention facilities before? If so, why do you need another tour?"

Candidate Obama had promised greater transparency. His own supporters on the left were deflated by the move to limit media coverage. In an interview with Fox, the ACLU said efforts to limit media coverage contradicted the administration's own pledges. "I think it's essential to keep pressing for access to the prisons," Anthony Romero told me outside of Guantánamo's high-security courthouse. "Whether the conditions of confinement are humane . . . taking the government's word for it is just not sufficient.

"It is more than a bit ironic that members of the press are

now being denied access to the camps when they had it before under President Bush."

Geoff Morrell was openly hostile at the Pentagon briefing when Fox Pentagon producer Justin Fishel asked for an explanation. "I'm not so sure the policy has changed," Morrell sniped. "If Fox is having a particular issue with getting an opportunity to go down there and see the detention facilities for the 100th or 150th time, I'd be happy to try to work with you to figure out an opportunity to do so, okay?"

When we followed up, he wasn't helpful either. In fact, members of the Pentagon press office, including Bryan Whitman, who was in charge of press operations, tried to discourage Fox from broadcasting our report on the lack of transparency.

The incident culminated in a conference call between Whitman's deputy, Colonel Dave Lapan; Fox's Washington bureau manager; and Fox's managing editor, Bill Sammon. Lapan argued that our story was leaving the wrong impression. Sammon said he would review the script but nothing more. Our report went to air.

The same day that the Pentagon press office denied Fox access to the camps, Greek TV and a British newspaper were allowed into the camps for a tour. Lapan's statement that "sometimes it's the logistics piece of it and the number of people it takes to do these separate and distinct missions" rang hollow.

The statements from some members of the Pentagon press office seemed designed to discourage independent reporting. After a story on the military commissions that cited two well-placed sources who believed the process was on hold because there had been no movement on the *Cole* case in twelve months, the head of the Pentagon press office appeared to lean on me once again.

Bryan Whitman wrote in an e-mail, "I don't have the time or inclination to get into the pattern right now, but it is probably something that needs to be discussed soon. You are getting a reputation with Department officials that doesn't bode well for you or us quite frankly."

One day after our report on the lack of transparency hit air, my producer, Shayla Bezdrob, was having trouble. I was not with her at the live shot position, but she described how a half dozen guys wearing cargo pants and wraparound sunglasses, with empty holsters on their thighs, swarmed her. As she relayed the story to me, Bezdrob told the soldiers to stop taking pictures of her and the crew. "Can you *not*?" she asked. "What are you doing?"

Bezdrob said they claimed the pictures were meant to "document" the history of the military trials for the Defense Department.

Bezdrob said she was angry at what she considered an effort to intimidate us. She put her hands on her hips and told them politely to leave. It's never smart to mess with a reporter who cut her teeth on the siege of Sarajevo.

Not long after the demonstration, the administration transferred four Uighurs to Bermuda. If there was a connection between the Uighurs' "Hetler" sign and their newfound freedom, the White House wasn't saying.

In any event, Greg Craig, the president's personal lawyer at the time, escorted the men on a jet with leather seats.

It was surreal meeting the Uighurs at their new home, a modest pastel bungalow with a swimming pool on the northwest coast of Bermuda. They wore new clothes, including tan pants pulled high up around their waists.

The four men introduced themselves through a translator.

Though their English was poor, the Uighurs made one point clear. "I am not terrorist. I had not been terrorist and I will never be terrorist," one said.

After the brief introduction, which did not include shaking my hand, as I was a woman, we were led into their small living room. They answered our questions without hesitation.

"For the record, the men have never been members of al Qaeda? They have never met with Bin Laden?" I felt ridiculous even asking. What were they really going to say?

The men started laughing. Their translator giggled as she spoke. "They all said no membership in al Qaeda [and they] never met with Bin Laden."

In answering the obvious question—What was worse, life at Guantánamo or life in China?—the four men did not miss a beat.

"Of course, it's China," their interpreter gushed. "There's no guarantee for any human lives there."

I thought I recognized at least one of the Uighurs from the demonstration at Camp Iguana. I wondered if he was the detainee who had an old bullet wound that looked like Antarctica on his forearm. It was the "identifying characteristic" cited by the military censor to justify erasing our video of the demonstration.

Even before press access was limited by an administration that touted open government, there was a brazen attempt to censor the news. The review process at Guantánamo tested everyone's patience. It was time-consuming. Every frame of video and every photo was examined for security breaches before it left the island. The military censor paced around the press center with his camouflage hat and dark sunglasses on.

The list of rules was seventeen pages long. No faces or distinguishing characteristics that identify detainees. So shooting video of detainees using walkers because they were so old was out. Taking pictures of shorelines or horizons was not allowed either. It apparently provided too much information on structures and locations. Had no one at the Navy base or the Pentagon heard of Google Earth?

My cameraman, Geoff Doyle, an old pro from NBC News, was getting frustrated. Who could blame him? He was going through frame by frame with a military censor who was determined to kill our tape.

I asked Geoff to take a break and step outside. When he balked, I insisted. After Geoff left, I took my military contact aside. We huddled in a dark corner of the hangar near the soda machine and the dispenser for calling cards. "Look," I said, "we've been working together a long time and I don't want you to have any surprises. My instructions from Fox are not to hand over the tape under any circumstances. I have been told the tape cannot be edited. I have been told not to leave the island without the tape. Period."

My contact looked nervous. I felt nervous too. At the time, my husband was deployed in Afghanistan. I didn't know how I'd fudge more time with the babysitters if I had to stay at the base.

I had my contact's attention. It was time to deliver the final blow.

"I will get on the air and report the administration that promised full transparency is now trying to destroy our videotape where the detainees call President Obama a communist. That is the story I will report on the first day." I paused. "It gets much worse on the second day."

About an hour later, my contact and the military censor

returned to the press workspace. The censor announced that the bullet wound was not an identifiable characteristic after all. They are all battlefield jihadists, he said.

As we left the island, with tape in hand, Geoff the cameraman asked the obvious question. "Was that really the advice you got from Fox New York?"

"Hell no," I said, and smiled.

. . .

In July 2010, a year after the military censor tried and failed to destroy our videotape of the demonstration, press access to the camps was slowly improving. I was hard-pressed to say why. I wondered if the administration had finally thrown in the towel on closing Guantánamo. We were now six months past the president's self-imposed deadline for shuttering the camps in January 2010.

The beat reporters were allowed into the camps but there were no tours of Camp Iguana, the site of the demonstration. The biggest change was the quality of life for detainees. It was on an upward trajectory.

As we entered the perimeter gate at Camp 4, we could see a detainee dumping out dirt. He was actually gardening not twenty-five yards from where the president's executive order, announcing the intended closure of the camps, was posted on a bulletin board. The notice was badly bleached after eighteen months in the Cuban sun.

Camp 4 was open-air. "Highly compliant" detainees enjoyed "communal living" as they passed the time growing vegetables and fruit. They were avid soccer players.

There was a library too. It was a small but busy place.

Sketches by the detainees lined the pale hallways. Journalists could look at the art and take notes, but video and photos were not allowed. The sketches of sunsets and palm trees were not cleared by the military. With a straight face, our guide explained that the pictures might contain coded messages for terrorists.

If art wasn't enough, the detainees enjoyed popular literature like Harry Potter and the Twilight series. Why teen angst and unrequited love appealed to suspected al Qaeda members remained a mystery to others and me.

Inside some of the magazines, the women's faces, bare arms, and uncovered legs were scratched out with dark ink. Our military guide, who asked that his name and face not be shown, was eager to point it out.

Satellite TV was now common in most of the camps. More than a dozen stations were available, including Al Jazeera English as the detainees' twenty-four-hour news source. Even the World Cup was taped and played back for the men. "We give them a variety of things," Army lieutenant colonel Andrew McManus said. "We have a Tunisian station, a Libyan station, Omani, Kuwaiti . . . a variety of topics. Their primary things they like are news, sports, and nature. Nature shows are very popular so we try to pick those stations for all that."

The favorite show of alleged al Qaeda and Taliban members was the series about deep-sea fishing off the coast of Alaska called *Deadliest Catch*. No one could explain why. Nor could anyone explain why some detainees got riled up so easily.

"There are cultural differences, and there are many things that can agitate the population," Navy commander Jeff Hayhurst told journalists on an earlier tour. "Even a TV ad of a fully clothed female who was washing her arms, I believe it was the Palmolive commercial, just agitated them."

For a moment, let's take a step back and compare life for the detainees with conditions at a supermax prison in the United States. Granted, the detainees are alleged terrorists and inmates at the supermax are convicted terrorists, but the contrast is stark. Is this really what justice amounted to?

While the Guantánamo crew enjoyed phone calls and Skype with relatives in Yemen and Saudi Arabia, convicted terrorists at the supermax in Colorado watched black-and-white TV's with 12-inch screens.

Courses for inmates like Zacarias Moussaoui, the convicted al Qaeda conspirator, or the Unabomber, Ted Kaczynski, were played on closed-circuit television. Guantánamo detainees were offered a new and popular seminar called "Life Skills." "We took our core class, which was Arabic/English, Pashto/English, and art, and added a life skills, which is a seminar," Colonel McManus said matter-of-factly. "That is based to give them skills they need when they leave here."

We also learned that personal finance as well as health and well-being were taught.

By the summer of 2010, the camps felt like a Holiday Inn Express—maybe a Marriott. Every dietary need was met. Outdoor exercise equipment was installed. President Obama had brought change the detainees could believe in.

· · ·

Ibrahim al-Qosi was from Sudan. He appeared well mannered and well groomed. I never saw him shackled. Al-Qosi was a longtime friend and aide to Osama bin Laden. They first met in the African nation, a onetime safe haven for the al Qaeda leader.

While the U.S. national security apparatus referred to al-Qosi as the first terrorist to plead guilty under the Obama administration, he was more commonly known as Bin Laden's cook. Al-Qosi was never described as an operational planner, an explosives expert, or a recruiter.

The military commissions point man for the press was Joe DellaVedova. He was pleasant to have around, and his encyclopedic knowledge of the cases came in handy. We shared the same workspace near the portable bathrooms. Joe worked hard and he worked late.

On the day of al-Qosi's hearing, Joe's advice was simple: Pay close attention. Most of the plea agreement would be read in open court. Joe said a court transcript might not be available for weeks—maybe never. It was a one-shot deal.

Al-Qosi sat quietly next to his lawyers. He listened to the interpreter through headphones. He spoke only a few times, to answer simple questions.

Under the rules, the military judge must be satisfied that the evidence supports a guilty plea. The judge must also be satisfied that the defendant, soon to be a convicted terrorist, understands the deal and enters it willingly.

Joe was right. Fresh information about Bin Laden and his lifestyle was sprinkled throughout the hearing. After Bin Laden was pushed out of Sudan, al-Qosi followed his friend. He eventually made the trek across the Afghan border. When al-Qosi finally arrived, he settled in as Bin Laden's head of the kitchen.

Bin Laden eventually moved his compound, called the Star of Jihad, to Kandahar, Afghanistan. It took half a dozen taxis to get everyone moving. I could only conclude that an Afghan taxi was not like an American taxi. Each one carried about fifteen passengers. When Bin Laden traveled, he rode separately in a truck with armed guards.

The Bin Laden camps were well organized. There was a compound for singles and another compound for married families. There were several apartments, each with two rooms and one bathroom. There were no phones. It was spartan living. Apparently, al-Qosi was in his element cooking for the bachelor crowd.

The camps were social places. Mullah Omar, the head of the Taliban, liked to pop in on holidays. Abu Hafs or Mohammed Atef also paid his respects. Atef allegedly played a leading role in the bombing of the U.S. embassies in Africa. In November 2001, Atef was one of the first high-value targets to be killed in Afghanistan. The court testimony implied that al-Qosi worked overtime to cater to their needs.

Al-Qosi was portrayed as a loyal person. While he didn't know about the attacks in advance, he stayed with his boss after 9/11. It was a decision that would cost him dearly. His defense team argued, unsuccessfully, that the Sudanese national was in it for the paycheck and not Bin Laden's friendship.

A month before 9/11, Bin Laden suddenly left Kandahar and fled to Tora Bora. According to court testimony, Bin Laden left behind at least a hundred followers, presumably to be slaughtered once the U.S. strikes ensued. He also left al-Qosi behind. Bin Laden did not repay his longtime aide's friendship or loyalty.

Lots of things at Guantánamo were screwy. The plea deal was no different. We knew the number was low for the plea deal, but the Al Arabiya satellite news network reported that it amounted to a cap of two more years.

In a matter of weeks, a military jury was called into service. Based on the evidence presented at a sentencing hearing, the jury gave al-Qosi fourteen years for conspiracy and providing material support to al Qaeda.

Under the commissions, the plea deal was weighted in favor of the convicted terrorist. Al-Qosi would get the lesser of the two sentences. If the Al Arabiya reporter was right, the Sudanese cook would be on his way home in the summer of 2012—before the president's first term was over.

The case of another detainee, a twenty-four-year-old Canadian named Omar Khadr, was running along a parallel track. At the age of fifteen, he was picked up on the battlefield in Afghanistan. More than a third of Khadr's life had been spent in U.S. military custody.

For the Obama administration, it was a bad case with which to inaugurate the new commissions. It was ugly politically. Critics said the Obama administration would forever have the distinction of trying a "child soldier" who was introduced to al Qaeda by his father.

The Khadrs were an unusual group. The Canadians were sometimes referred to mockingly as the first family of al Qaeda. Young Omar's father was reported to be a moneyman for the terrorist network before he was shot dead by Pakistani security forces.

The son was accused of throwing a hand grenade over a wall and killing U.S. Special Forces sergeant Chris Speer. Speer was the team's medic. When he was hit, the others did what they could to stabilize him.

Khadr was badly wounded in the firefight, too, but somehow American forces managed to save him. Now he was on trial for murder. A former chief prosecutor at Guantánamo, retired colonel Lawrence Morris, said the "child soldier" argument was bogus. "In America, if Sergeant Speer was walking out of some Applebee's in Fayetteville, North Carolina, and some fifteen-year-old went out and murdered him, you can be quite sure that as a juvenile he would be held accountable in adult court."

There were two sides to Khadr. In a Web video, shot by al Qaeda as propaganda, the teenager made a crude bomb. It was the type of device used in roadside attacks that killed and maimed U.S. soldiers.

In another video, released by his defense team, Khadr was shown crying like a baby in front of his interrogators. He complained about his wounds. He alleged poor medical treatment. After he was allegedly threatened with rape and death, Khadr's attorneys claimed, he confessed to throwing the grenade.

The judge ruled Khadr's confessions were admissible even though one of his interrogators was convicted of abusing detainees in a separate case. The Canadian's attorneys called the decision "an embarrassment" for the U.S. government. Khadr would eventually plead guilty and get a cap of eight years. Under the plea deal, analysts expected him to be sent home to Canada in one year. Parole could be around the corner.

Perhaps it was disgust at the relatively light sentence coupled with the loss of her husband that led Speer's widow to tell Khadr her children "didn't deserve to have their father taken by someone like you." Tabitha Speer added, "You will forever be a murderer in my eyes."

On the flight from Andrews Air Force Base in Virginia to Guantánamo, one face in the crowd was new yet familiar. It took me a moment to recognize David Iglesias in military uniform. Iglesias was one of the eight U.S. attorneys fired by the Bush administration. In his case, the firing was unrelated to the war on terror.

Now a U.S. attorney who was thrown under the bus by the last administration was a spokesman and lawyer for the revamped military commissions under President Obama. It was more than a bit ironic.

When I asked how it felt to be back in the spotlight, Iglesias answered: "It's great to be back in uniform. I started my legal career as a Navy JAG officer twenty-six years ago and I have a lot of respect for Navy JAGs. There's a lot of talent at DOD [Defense Department] and DOJ [Department of Justice], but whoever gets the call will be very fortunate because 9/11 represents the most significant criminal case in American history."

As for who should get the case, the military or federal prosecutors, Iglesias played it safe. "It is a political call. I'm not going to wade into those waters."

We finished the interview. As I walked away I imagined the symbolism of someone like Iglesias leading a high-profile case like that of the men accused of plotting the attack on the USS *Cole*, or of the 9/11 suspects.

That summer former FBI director Louis Freeh and a former chief judge for the U.S. Court of Appeals for the Armed Forces, Eugene R. Sullivan, offered a clever way out of the problem. Like many brilliant ideas, it was surprisingly simple on paper. Putting it into practice was quite another matter.

Freeh and Sullivan wrote in the *Washington Post* that combining the security of the Guantánamo court with the perceived advantages of the federal, or Article III, courts was worth a try. There was no political will to move the trials to the United States. And with a quick and dirty statute, Congress could expand the "territorial jurisdiction" of any federal trial venue.

They also argued that the commissions were seen as second-tier justice. By trying alleged terrorists like war criminals, the United States would be lending credibility to their cause. This argument fell into the "treat them like common criminals" category. And let's not forget the money. The trials were going to cost in excess of $200 million—the projected cost for security at a Manhattan trial.

. . .

Judge, jury, and executioner: it sounds very un-American. But by the spring of 2010, it was the Obama administration's strategy for dealing with Anwar al-Awlaki. Sources were confirming reports that the White House had authorized a kill or capture order for the cleric. It meant that al-Awlaki was the first American on the CIA's hit list. Every time I saw a certain FBI agent or senior counterterrorism official, he gloated. "He [al-Awlaki] won't be around by Easter" stretched into "He will be done by the end of the year."

The authorization to kill revealed another inconsistency in the Obama administration's strategy. The White House wanted to give the 9/11 suspects the same constitutional rights as U.S. citizens in federal courts. The finest legal defense on the planet was available to Khalid Sheikh Mohammed and others. More important, the defendants enjoyed the presumption of innocence.

How did you square that strategy with the stated goal of assassinating an American citizen in a foreign country? The administration was eliminating an American when no federal indictment was public. When asked at the White House briefing to square the two strategies, press secretary Robert Gibbs punted to the Justice Department. A spokesman for Holder had no answer either.

The CIA kill or capture order made me stop and think

about the power the U.S. government wields. Al-Awlaki was a key player in the case of Ali al-Timimi, who was serving life in prison. You may remember that al-Awlaki showed up unexpectedly at al-Timimi's house with a government witness in the fall of 2002. There were unusual connections between al-Awlaki and an FBI agent in the case. And al-Awlaki exchanged e-mails with Major Nidal Hasan.

Wouldn't it be better for an American citizen to testify in an American court in the prosecution of another American citizen? I asked myself. Wouldn't it be more American to give al-Awlaki a trial rather than silence him?

Why did the U.S. government, and an administration that espoused transparency, want to kill the cleric who held so many answers?

. . . .

CHAPTER 5

GUESS WHO'S COMING TO LUNCH

The Capital Grille

Washington, D.C.

Late March 2010

1930 hours

I t is still unbearably cold and wet as I pull out of the underground parking lot near the corner of North Capitol and
E Street NW. The blizzard of February 2010, more commonly know as "Snowmageddon," is now behind us.

I am on my way to meet a longtime counterterrorism contact.
We've talked about Fort Hood and the e-mail traffic between
Major Nidal Hasan and the American cleric Anwar al-Awlaki.
We've talked at length about the evolving threat.

To be clear, my contact is not a leaker by nature. He does

me favors from time to time by confirming that the intelligence I have is good. He gently tells me when I am heading in the wrong direction.

As I make the quick turn down Louisiana Avenue and then a right onto Pennsylvania, the Capitol appears bathed in white light. I consider the next step in my strategy. We are four months into our investigative documentary for *Fox News Reporting,* and my two primary goals are still unmet. We don't have the Hasan e-mails. We don't have the al-Awlaki mug shots either.

To those who pass my old red Volkswagen, I am the crazy woman behind the wheel, with gloves on, talking to herself. Should I warm him up first with a few drinks? Or is it better to cut to the chase? After all, we have been friends for years. I pause. But can a reporter and a federal investigator ever really be friends?

I am up and out of the car and past the decorative lions that stand guard at the Capital Grille's main entrance. At Sixth and Pennsylvania Avenue NW, the restaurant is a stone's throw from Congress. It is a place where information is exchanged over steaks and generous drinks.

It is warm inside. I can see my old friend near the end of the bar. He's drinking by himself. I respect that. People without vices, especially in the intelligence world, make me nervous.

I hop up onto the barstool. We go through the usual motions over who will buy the drinks. We agree to pay for our own. He's on his second bourbon. I am on my first glass of Cabernet.

"So, my friend, I saw the audio message you got from Awlaki. Impressive." He is looking down at his drink as he talks.

"I got the audiotape on Wednesday, the tenth." I try to be matter-of-fact about the timing. I know he's interested, but in this cat-and-mouse game, I don't want to appear overeager.

He tells me the timing is impossible. I double-check my BlackBerry, then hold it out in front of him like a piece of evidence. "Actually, I got a sample of the tape about thirty-five seconds long right here. See the date? They wanted thirty thousand dollars for the entire tape—eleven minutes—but Fox doesn't pay. By Saturday, I managed to get the full Web link and the password."

"Well, my friend"—he looks up at me—"it looks like you got the tape before we did. I am a little concerned about that. You apparently have a source we don't know about. I would be very interested in learning more."

This is my chance for the grand bargain. I want the mug shots of Anwar al-Awlaki for the prostitution charges in San Diego and Washington, D.C. My friend wants to know more about how I got the audiotape. It seems a reasonable swap. "What do you say, I help you and you help me?" I clearly have his attention, but not in a good way.

"What's the big deal?" I continue. "They are booking photos. They are public property. I can get Nick Nolte's or Charlie Sheen's mug shot but I can't get Awlaki's? Come on, it doesn't come close to classified information."

"I just don't know if I can get them for you." He is now looking down again. I know that's not a good sign.

Since our investigation began after Fort Hood, I've learned that the mere mention of al-Awlaki's name to a government official can be a conversation killer. Now I can't keep a lid on my frustration. "Okay. I want the mug shots and I want all eighteen e-mails exchanged between Major Hasan and Awlaki."

My friend looks genuinely upset. Now I feel bad. I just want the pictures. I don't want to blow up our working relationship.

"There is no way I can get those e-mails," he says. "But maybe I can find out who is blocking the mug shots."

"You are not listening to me!" I lean toward him from the barstool. "I don't get the U.S. government. When you are handed an opportunity—on a platter—to discredit this guy Awlaki, you can't even take it? Do you want to win or what?"

. . .

On May 1, 2011, President Obama announced that Osama bin Laden was dead. U.S. Navy Seals killed the al Qaeda leader at his compound near the Pakistani capital Islamabad. The initial intelligence thread came in 2003 from the controversial CIA interrogation program. It was developed over an eight-year time frame.

To understand the future, we must briefly return to the past. We connected again with Charlie Allen, who spent forty-seven years in the CIA and three at Homeland Security leading intelligence. He was the first person to publicly identify al-Awlaki, his violent message, and his blog as a threat to U.S. national security.

In the fog after 9/11, Allen said, the intelligence community was doing a lot of heavy lifting. "Back in 2001, 2002, I took no time off and worked every day for months on end."

Nine years later, as the threat evolved, Allen believed more Americans would be recruited to al Qaeda's cause. "I think we'll have growth in extremism. And there will be more Americans who've listened to the siren call of this extremist jihad."

Charlie said he was talking about jihad not as a personal struggle for someone's soul, but as a global movement. The target, he predicted, would be Western governments, and primarily that of the United States.

Good analysts are never fond of speculating. But when pushed, Allen said the American recruit of the future probably looked like Najibullah Zazi, who confessed to an al Qaeda plot aimed at the New York subway system in 2009. "It looks more like a guy, like Zazi from Colorado, who quietly plotted to attack the mass transportation in New York. . . . He flew under the radar."

Zazi was a legal permanent resident, or LPR. He traveled overseas to the tribal areas of Pakistan for training. Adnan Shukrijumah, at the time al Qaeda's senior operations planner, allegedly directed him. It was not surprising. Shukrijumah was cut from the same cloth as Zazi. He was born overseas and raised in the United States.

At the time of this writing, there was a $5 million reward for information leading to Shukrijumah's capture. He'd been a fugitive for a long time in both Afghanistan and the tribal areas of Pakistan.

"As the ranks have become depleted, here we have another American who is now allegedly the external operations chief for al Qaeda. That's a big job."

It was a big job, but as Allen noted, most who held the position wound up dead.

Allen was not surprised that the operative behind the failed bombing on Times Square in May 2010 was also an American and a follower of al-Awlaki. Like Zazi and Shukrijumah, Faisal Shahzad was also a longtime resident of the U.S.

Based on the intelligence he had access to, Allen said 2006 was the turning point. Al Qaeda's Abu Ubaida al-Masri made a conscious and concerted effort to identify new recruits who were hard to detect. "They changed . . . strategy in 2006. They began to train substantial numbers of North Americans."

While Allen didn't come out and say it, the implication was clear. The post-9/11 scrutiny of young Muslim men from countries like Pakistan, Afghanistan, and Saudi Arabia put al Qaeda on notice.

"We have an open society. Americans travel broadly, internationally, by the millions. . . . We'll not ever be perfect and we can never say the country will not be attacked again, because in my view it will be. But what we have to do is work hard to mitigate that threat . . . by going on the offense and disrupting al Qaeda."

Shahzad also fit the pattern Allen described. In its sentencing memo, the government described a propaganda video made by Shahzad and the Pakistani Taliban who trained him. Presumably, they planned to release the tape once the bomb went off in Times Square. Instead, the bomb fizzled and Shahzad was picked up as he tried to flee the country.

According to court documents, the video showed Shahzad taking pride in the plot to kill countless civilians in May 2010. In a haunting statement, he urged others to follow his lead. "I also want to inform my brothers [*sic*] Muslims abroad living abroad [*sic*] that it is not difficult at all to wage an attack on the West, and specifically in the U.S., and completely defeat them."

Shahzad was also a fan and follower of al-Awlaki. He collected his CDs. The former financial analyst from Connecticut was vulnerable. "He had economic difficulties. He had difficulties with his personal life. And he became more pious and more religious and he corresponded like others with Anwar Awlaki." Allen explored the connection further. "It's not surprising. Again, this is an individual who can really touch . . . Americans . . . Muslim Americans . . . people who have come to this country who are alienated. Who are beginning to have strong feelings about a global jihad."

It was inevitable, Allen said, that Americans would rise through the ranks, as al Qaeda was in a strategic decline. The efforts by the United States and its allies were paying off. "I didn't realize that he [al-Awlaki] would reach that level of importance. But as you know over half of al Qaeda's leaders are dead or captured, so there's always room at the top, it seems."

The number of homegrown cases was rising. A background document produced by the Justice Department showed forty-one cases of category 1 offenses—the most serious cases, with a direct connection to international terrorism—between January 2009 and August 2010 that involved U.S. citizens.

"I think we'll get some more cases," Charlie commented. "I don't know that they're going to rise sharply, but the numbers will grow over time. We haven't peaked."

When I asked what al-Awlaki's future looked like, Charlie was definite. "Let's hope not much."

"Not much? You think it ends soon for him?"

I was referring to the CIA's kill or capture order for the cleric. Charlie let the question lie. He probably knew a lot more from his longtime CIA contacts than he wanted to reveal. "Well, let's see what history brings."

I pushed a little harder. "Will he have a page in history or will he be just a footnote in history?"

"I view him as having half a page in history—someone who was very willing to put his own Muslims at risk. You've got to remember, most of the people murdered in Iraq or Afghanistan or elsewhere have been Muslims."

Charlie said al-Awlaki was riding the wave of popularity generated by the global jihadist movement. He had a narcissistic personality. In the short term, he prospered, but the years to follow would be different.

"Is there anything that you want to add that I haven't asked?"

"No, I think not." Charlie paused. "I think Anwar al-Awlaki does not have a bright future."

. . .

On 9/11, General Michael Hayden, the first intelligence officer to attain the rank of four-star general in the Air Force, was director of the National Security Agency. Hayden combined sharp intellect with compassion. It was a rare and prized combination that would eventually lead him to the CIA, which he oversaw between 2006 and 2009.

When the first plane struck, Hayden canceled his morning meeting at the NSA and sent home all nonessential personnel. Despite his order, about a quarter of the fifteen-thousand-strong workforce remained. Late that morning, he phoned his wife, Jeanine, and asked her to find their kids. Within two hours of the attack, George Tenet, then CIA director, confirmed with Hayden that Bin Laden was behind the strikes.

"George called me," Hayden recalled. "It was probably eleven thirty. [Tenet asked,] 'Are you getting anything?'"

Hayden said, "Yeah, it's al Qaeda."

Tenet responded, "Yeah, we know. But you're getting stuff." He was referring to the signals intelligence the NSA was picking up.

Hayden said al Qaeda was reveling in the murder of nearly three thousand Americans. "Yeah, they've started to get a little congratulatory."

At dusk on 9/11, Hayden went to the NSA's counterterrorism center. The staff, he said, were mostly Arab Americans. They were traumatized. "As I walked in the logistics forces, as I told you, it was about dusk and they were on the upper floors in one of the high-rises. They were putting up blackout curtains. They all feared a follow-on attack was imminent. Blackout curtains in eastern Maryland!"

Hayden was now a principal at the Chertoff Group, a highly selective consulting company founded by former Homeland Security secretary Michael Chertoff, specializing in risk management and security. Hayden's office was down the hall from that of Charlie Allen, another principal. I waved and exchanged greetings with Charlie as I passed.

Michael Chertoff was Homeland Security secretary from 2005 to 2009. I interviewed him more than a half dozen times. He was one of the first outspoken proponents of risk management. You couldn't protect everything all of the time, he used to say. You had to decide what the most catastrophic attacks would look like and block them.

While not ruling out a large-scale attack in the future, Hayden said the United States intelligence community was better at detecting plots. "They are less likely—not because they are less desired by the enemy. But the enemy is less capable. I'm being flip, but I can't rule out the possibility that we've actually been successful for the last eight years."

Hayden said spectacular attacks were more complex. They took more time. There were lots of loose ends to follow. "We are good enough now that [you] grab one of the threads, you start pulling it—pretty soon you got a fur ball, then you got yourself a plot, and you begin to take action against it."

What concerned Hayden were commando-style attacks like the one in Mumbai, India, in 2008. About a dozen terrorists, young men armed with guns and with cell phones for communication, stormed multiple targets, including the train station and the majestic Oberoi Hotel. By the time the three-day siege ended, more than 170 were dead. The plot was directed by a Pakistani group, not well known in the West, called Lashkar-e-Taiba. They were determined to free Kashmir from Indian control.

"The new flavor is self-radicalized and low-threshold," Hayden said, summing up the threat picture. "As bad as it [Mumbai] was in and of itself, it was really frightening to us because here was an attack by about a dozen people with automatic weapons and cell phones. Not overly complex but it had the kind of macro, political, and economic impact that formerly you could get with only mass-destruction attacks against iconic targets."

The Mumbai attack was doubly troubling for U.S. intelligence officials because an American, David Headley, played a pivotal role in the plot. Headley was a Pakistani American who also gamed the system. As reported by ProPublica, an investigative journalism project, Headley was a former drug dealer and an informant for the Drug Enforcement Administration whose wives and close contacts warned U.S. authorities about his activities six times before December 2008.

Headley made at least five trips to Mumbai to case the hotel and other sites. He also identified the landing zones along the water for the terrorists who arrived by boat.

Headley's name and that of al Qaeda operative Ilyas Kashmiri would surface again in connection with the fall 2010 terror alerts in Europe. It was Headley's contact with known al Qaeda operatives in Britain that led to his undoing.

Once it was alerted by the British, the FBI arrested Headley in the fall of 2009. According to Headley's plea agreement, which covered Mumbai and a plot to attack a Danish newspaper, Kashmiri told him he had active supporters and cells in Europe who could help Headley launch a Mumbai-style attack on the Continent.

Hayden agreed that the growing number of Americans in terrorist plots would make the job more difficult. "The profile appears to be young alienated Islamic males. And to be fair too, I understand that identifying them as Islamic is kind of a third rail politically here." Hayden punctuated his assessment with a joke. "We are not being attacked by Irish nuns."

Hayden predicted that the policy debate would focus on substantive issues in the future, for example, how much do the American people want foreign intelligence mixed with domestic intelligence and law enforcement data?

To illustrate the point, Hayden took out a piece of paper and drew a rough chart. In the middle was a line. Above it, he drew a series of check marks. Each one represented a major attack like 9/11, the liquid explosive bomb plot of 2006 that led to the three-ounce rule for passenger carry-on luggage, and the so-called Bojinka plot—another one of Khalid Sheikh Mohammed's sinister ideas—to blow up twelve jets over the Pacific Ocean. Hayden said the intelligence community probably had the tools it needed to prevent similar attacks in the future, but he emphasized that there were no guarantees.

But the pressing problem was small-scale attacks. He pointed below the line on the chart. The check marks included Fort Hood; the recruitment center shooting in Arkansas; Najibullah Zazi, who tried to bomb the New York subway; and Headley. "What I would argue for is political leadership saying,

'Look, I can push the line here.'" Hayden took his pen and ran it left to right to show where the lower threshold might be. "But I'm not, because you and I know we don't want it to be here."

Hayden said the decision not to lower the threshold had consequences. More small-scale attacks were likely. But, he argued, this was an acceptable long-term strategy. "The new flavor of attacks are less complicated, less well organized, less likely to succeed, and they will have less lethality should they succeed. They are just going to be more numerous. That is a successful counterterrorism policy. That is a measure of our success."

The Somali affiliate al-Shabaab was a lingering worry for Hayden and others. He questioned whether the July 2010 double suicide bombing in Kampala, Uganda, was a red flag. Al-Shabaab had claimed responsibility for the attacks. It coincided with the World Cup final. The dead included spectators in a rugby club and an Ethiopian restaurant. Al-Shabaab actively recruited American citizens. Was the group no longer content to be a regional player in East Africa? Would its recruits turn their violent acts on the United States?

"Shabaab goes regional—that's new. . . . Is that the first sign of them going regional and beyond, or is it simply the high water where they could settle a 'one-off' case, a local grudge outside the borders of Somalia? It bears watching. Frankly, [I'm] more pessimistic than optimistic. I think it's the former—trying to get more global reach from the Horn of Africa."

On this subject, Hayden provided needed context. The drone campaign in the tribal areas of Pakistan, begun by Bush and continued by Obama, put the al Qaeda leadership under pressure. To the surprise of some analysts, al Qaeda core stayed in the neighborhood. The al Qaeda franchises in Yemen and

Somalia, Hayden noted, did not become safe havens for the leadership. Instead, they stepped up. They developed plots of their own.

Al Qaeda in Yemen was one of the first out of the box, with the attempted Christmas Day bombing in December 2009. Would al Qaeda in North Africa follow? For example, in the fall of 2010, the French authorities and European intelligence officials were extremely worried. Reports circulated that a woman of Algerian descent, an alleged suicide bomber, was on her way to France.

As of this writing, one of my most trusted open-source intelligence contacts, David, started sending new information about al Qaeda in Nigeria. Umar Farouk Abdulmutallab, who wore the underwear bomb on Christmas Day, was from Nigeria. It didn't look like a coincidence.

Hayden's analysis hit close to home. My husband, J.D., recently told me that his next deployment was scheduled for 2012. Once again, our lives as a military family were impacted by the threat. It made me sad to think about the kids missing their dad again.

Hayden said the terrorist movements of the future would be fueled by the same kind of youth alienation found in criminal gangs. The recruits would be disaffected and rootless, looking for an identity, a place to belong.

When Hayden was CIA director, he said, his analysts downplayed the significance of the Internet. They believed contact between the individual and the recruiter was key. In the case of Umar Farouk Abdulmutallab, a senior official with knowledge of the case told me in August 2010 that Anwar al-Awlaki met with the young Nigerian in Yemen, taught him how to avoid

Western security and surveillance, and hooked him up with the bomb maker.

Now, given cases like Fort Hood, Hayden was rethinking the assessment from his days as CIA director. "The most important element in any recruitment was the personal contact, and while the Web may have been useful, fundamentally it was the personal contact. It's the mentoring thing. I don't know if that was true then but it seems to be less true now as some people, Hasan for example, seem to have just done it purely with the Internet."

. . .

Lieutenant Colonel Tony Shaffer was covert for years. He had so many cover names that he couldn't remember them all. After 9/11, he went into the belly of the beast, Afghanistan. Still in the Army Reserves, Shaffer worked for a small Washington, D.C., think tank, the Center for Advanced Defense Studies, where he focused on the threat of nuclear weapons falling into the hands of terrorists. He said he concentrates on "ground delivery through unconventional methods such as delivery through pleasure craft, via a [cargo] container, things which a conventional military would not consider as a part of warfare."

Like Allen and Hayden, Shaffer predicted that future operatives would include more Americans. Or at least, they would blend into the crowd. "The threat of the future is going to be someone who looks a lot more like us—in that the radicals have recognized that America is a lot more vigilant, that the 9/11 attacks, if nothing else, did make people wake up."

All of the 9/11 hijackers were foreign. They didn't understand the culture. They thought a mass-casualty attack on the United States would lead to widespread upheaval and a change in our political system. They were wrong. To survive, al Qaeda was forced to change.

With al Qaeda's emphasis on American and Western recruits, Shaffer said, profiling was more important than ever. Profiling went a lot deeper than skin color, than stereotypes like young Muslim men. Shaffer said an individual's actions, and his ideas and who shared them, were paramount. Shaffer alluded to Major Hasan, who sought out al-Awlaki for spiritual guidance. "The Major Hasan thing is something we have to be very cognizant of," Shaffer insisted. "This tendency for political correctness will get us killed."

Connecting the dots needed to happen faster, he said. We had to get smarter about detecting the radicalization process earlier. And once we detected a threatening individual through actions or associations, we needed to look faster at his past, to understand how the radicalization happened. "We cannot be afraid of looking at what the Defense Department calls 'U.S. person information,'" Shaffer said. The "U.S. person issue" restricts the use and retention of information on U.S. citizens or legal residents for intelligence purposes.

The lieutenant colonel spoke from experience. He was part of a controversial pre-9/11 Special Operations data-mining project called "Able Danger." Some of its members claimed to have identified the lead hijacker, Mohammed Atta, a year before the attacks. At least one analyst knew him under an alias, Mohammed al-Sayed.

While the Defense Department disputed the claim that Atta had been flagged as a threat, it did destroy the data, 2.5

terabytes, over the U.S. person issue. "I think it is lunacy that information which is openly available on any individual . . . on the Internet, that there would be some expectation of privacy."

Shaffer said objectives are also important to the profile. Al Qaeda and its affiliates have a track record of doing what they promise. "They have been very consistent. In their philosophy, they have to warn their enemy of what they are going to do. If you recall the 9/11 attacks, Bin Laden did these missives talking about the fact that he was going to attack us."

Shaffer expected people like the American cleric al-Awlaki to adopt a similar strategy. "I think you're going to have some kind of fundamental level of warning from people like Awlaki who feel this is a religious effort," Shaffer suggested. "Therefore requiring them to adhere to their warped, very clearly defined, in their world, definition of jihad."

While linkages through family or other contacts to Pakistan, Afghanistan, the Arabian Peninsula, and East Africa still mattered, Shaffer was on the same page as many analysts. Al Qaeda was aiming for recruits from Middle America. Whether it would succeed was another matter.

In July 2010, the highly anticipated al Qaeda Web magazine *Inspire* went online. A second edition was published three months later. Al Qaeda in Yemen was targeting a broader Western audience. "They [al Qaeda] want to have people who are essentially misfits, people who are fed up with our society, who don't feel connected," Shaffer explained. Al Qaeda would offer them a sense of belonging to something bigger. Shaffer, like the half dozen members of the radicalization unit we met in chapter 3, said that al Qaeda was now a movement, a set of ideas. The Internet didn't make people do things, but it was one of the drivers. "They can belong. They are needed. They are wanted. . . . Frankly, because of the Internet and the way social media works, they [al Qaeda] will be mining them."

FBI director Robert Mueller testified to Congress in September 2010 that American recruits were better connected and, as a result, were better operators. Shaffer took the analysis a step further. Adding Americans to terrorist plots, especially a nuclear plot, could, he claimed, be devastating. "You have to have insiders who can do three things for you: Help get a weapon in, help set it up, and help detonate it. There is something called a 'PAL' [permissive action link], which is the control on a nuclear weapon. And most of the PAL experts are U.S. citizens."

Shaffer predicted that if a terrorist group obtained a nuclear device, the former Soviet Union or Pakistan would be the source. Because its conventional forces were run-down, he said, Russia had reinstituted tactical nuclear weapons as part of its overall strategy. Shaffer said these "forward deployed" weapons were more accessible and more vulnerable. They had the potential to fall into the wrong hands.

In Pakistan, Shaffer said, a stated goal of the Taliban and al Qaeda was to obtain Pakistani nukes and use them against the United States. "There is no reason to believe they are not going to do it. There have been at least seven credible attempts within the past two years by al Qaeda and Taliban elements to obtain access to nuclear weapons."

While suitcase nukes have been hyped as the likely threat, Shaffer said they were unreliable. The fissile material degraded rapidly, and there was a relatively small amount of it. A "dirty bomb," which is a device that combines nuclear material with conventional explosives, was more likely, he thought. It was sometimes referred to as a "weapon of mass hysteria" because it caused panic without killing large numbers of people.

In his interview, Shaffer lived up to his track record for bucking conventional thinking. It would be easier, he said, to bring in a large weapon. A four-hundred-pound nuke, about the size of a refrigerator, would be more reliable than something that could fit in a suitcase. And there were easy ways to move it. "To me the most likely scenario is a pleasure craft up on the rivers into a waterway. . . . Coast Guard has admitted through several recent studies that they do not have a good handle on security on the waterways—that could be one of our vulnerabilities." Shaffer's manner was direct. "I do believe that is potentially [the] most viable method should a nuclear weapon fall into the wrong hands."

Shaffer predicted that Washington, D.C., New York, and Los Angeles were the most desirable targets. "That's the danger of having this new generation of terrorists who understand how to hurt us. The combination of individuals who understand our culture, who understand how things work, combined with more lethal, much more lethal weapons could actually devastate this country in ways that 9/11 will look like a picnic."

• • •

If Shaffer's view of the future was ominous, one of the country's leading experts on cybersecurity said the United States was already under attack.

"How likely do you think a cyberattack supported by a terrorist group is against the U.S.?" I asked.

"A certitude." Dale Meyerrose did not hesitate. Meyerrose had more than thirty years of military service, retiring as a major general in the Air Force. His firsthand experience with the cyberthreat was well known. His last government job was overseeing intelligence sharing and technology acquisition for the director of national intelligence, the nation's top intelligence official. "Cyberterrorists use cybercrime in order to raise money, in order to move money, in order to do banking. That's already happened." While not going into specifics, Meyerrose said he'd seen it many times before. By the way he spoke, I concluded the details were still classified.

Meyerrose outlined two scenarios for future threats. The first scenario, he said, was more likely than the second. He predicted that cyberspace would be used to "prep the battlefield." The cyberattack would be a diversion, a secondary element to the main event. For example, in August 2008, while the U.S. election entered its final stretch, the former Soviet republic of Georgia came under attack. First the communications were hit, causing panic, which made it easier for Russian forces to move in.

In the second scenario, which Meyerrose felt was less likely, the physical attack would be the battlefield preparation for a large-scale cyberevent. Let's say a country has one or two TV stations. You put them under physical attack, with a series of car bombs, and this diverts attention while a denial-of-service attack is launched on banking and transportation systems.

At one point in the interview, Meyerrose took the conversation down a notch. I took note because it was unusual for him. By his own admission, Meyerrose was hard charging and high-energy. He joked about never drinking coffee.

He said the country and the government were stuck in a rut. We talked about "attacks" in a classic, old-fashioned way. He said it was different with the cyberthreat.

If I drew only one conclusion from our talk, Meyerrose urged me, I must explain the cyber footprint. It was totally misunderstood. It was not the same as someone's physical footprint. The blackout on the eastern seaboard in 2003 was a good example. One-third of the power generated for the North Atlantic region came out of Canada. The control element was in Ohio. It meant New York City's cyber footprint for energy reached into Canada and then back to the heartland. "If you want to affect the control systems for the power grid in New York you have to go to Cleveland, Ohio. If you want to affect the databases of the third-largest bank in the United States, which is headquartered in New York City, you have to go to Boulder, Colorado."

His definition of "cyber" boiled down to four words: man-made, virtual, borderless environment. Mobility was also important. Big decisions were increasingly made on hand-held devices, not in boardrooms. Social networking sites were commonplace at home and at work.

Our conversation drifted back to 9/11, as so many discussions of the future do. Meyerrose was at U.S. Northern Command in Colorado. "Saw a lot of stuff. I got a lot that I could say but I won't. We had a lot of the right people in the right spot as far as I'm concerned. We had people that did the best things in the interest of the country."

After decades, if not centuries, of focusing our military outward against foreign enemies, within forty-eight hours the U.S. military did something unthinkable. "If you'd been told prior to 9/11 that I was considering plans on how to use United States military planes to engage civilian airlines, you would have had me court-martialed." Meyerrose paused, reflecting on that day. "The skies were safe."

He felt Americans would become more prevalent in cyberplots. They were tailor-made for recruitment. They could hide in plain sight. Americans were also more attractive than foreign recruits because U.S. citizens have more protections under the law. In other words, the enemy was also using the very freedoms we were fighting to protect against us. "American citizens are the easiest to go after because they've set up their own barriers and hurdles that I can hide behind."

Meyerrose emphasized that the borderless nature of cyberspace blurred the lines separating foreign from domestic threats. He offered the example of a bad guy in Iraq talking to a bad guy in Afghanistan using a U.S.-owned Internet service provider. Too often, we were stuck in the past. "The business about borders and what's domestic and what's international and all those kinds of things, that's a 6.0 discussion and we are using 2.0 definitions and frames of reference."

Meyerrose, who had held some of the toughest technology and intelligence jobs, predicted a change in our thinking. We had to stop throwing up roadblocks that prevented us from looking at our own people. "In some cases, I'm not saying this for overemphasis, in some cases we're protecting people from an eighteenth-century mind-set in the twenty-first century. And the eighteenth-century mind-set is that we don't want our military or intelligence community to have any role in domestic affairs."

As I packed up my audio recorder and notebook, my mind drifted back to October 2001. With my overseas experience, Fox was planning to send me to Pakistan or Afghanistan. My shots were lined up. My malaria pills were bought and packed. At the last minute, my boss changed his mind. He sent me to Washington, D.C., instead to figure out "What the heck is this homeland security?" Fox said I would be gone for a couple of months. Nine years, a mortgage, a husband, two children, and a cat later, I was still in the nation's capital.

In those early days, the work was intense. It just kept coming. It was like drinking from a fire hose.

Meeting Governor Tom Ridge was one of my better memories. The former Pennsylvania governor was the right man at the right time. As the first White House adviser on homeland security and the first secretary for the Homeland Security Department, he took some knocks, but he kept moving forward.

At the fall 2010 "American Security Challenge," a forum that tries to match emerging technology that could secure the country with the defense or intelligence agencies, we hosted a discussion about the future. The focus was on cutting through the bureaucracy.

Governor Ridge summed up the challenge this way: "You cannot be secure unless your economy is strong. We're going to be at this for several generations. We have watches, but they have time."

Harvard Club
New York, New York
May 21, 2010
2100 hours

After a dinner of fish, we are walking back to the Harvard Club on West Forty-fourth Street. New York City is easing into summer. It is already hot and muggy. My good friend Kim Rosenberg, who is the executive producer of the *Fox Report with Shepard Smith*, is with me. Kim is extremely tall and attractive, with long dark hair that frames her face and big eyes.

As we roll up in front of the wide-screen TV, I am feeling nervous. Our six-month investigation into the cleric Anwar al-Awlaki is finally ready for prime time. Fox is taking a risk and broadcasting the special in the 9 p.m. time slot. This is Sean Hannity territory, and I am worried. Can a show about an American terrorist with hooker problems really hold the audience?

As the show opens, I am not watching the screen. I am watching Kim. Her standards are high. She likes to say she sees the screen like the average viewer. She likes things clear and simple.

As former Diplomatic Security agent Ray Fournier describes al-Awlaki's frequent run-ins with the law, Kim chimes in, "T.P. [Terror Pixie], I love that Awlaki was picking up hookers near the mosque, but I would have really hit people over the head with it. Like saying it twice." Kim pauses, then puts on her best announcer voice. "Thaaaat's right. See that mosque right there in the San Diego ghetto? It was just down the block that the holy man was picking up hos."

. . .

In the months immediately leading up to and after the documentary, all the threads were coming together. There was growing evidence that al-Awlaki was part of a support cell sent to the United States prior to 9/11.

The executive director of the 9/11 Commission, Philip Zelikow, rarely granted interviews, but he made an exception for our project. He said he was surprised that the media never picked up on al-Awlaki. The commission had done its best to question his connections to the 9/11 hijackers. "We put the spotlight on Awlaki about as brightly as we could, and as brightly as a government agency could," Zelikow told me at his home in Charlottesville, Virginia.

One question was never answered: Why would Khalid Sheikh Mohammed send two of his most experienced recruits, Nawaf al-Hazmi and Khalid al-Mihdhar, who spoke virtually no English, to a ghetto in Southern California unless there was someone there to meet them?

Mohdar Abdullah, a Yemeni like al-Awlaki, was the possible link between the two hijackers and the cleric. In February 2000, the 9/11 Commission Report suggested, Abdullah drove the two hijackers from Los Angeles to the San Diego ghetto. Given his fluency in Arabic and English, the commission concluded, he was "perfectly suited to assist the hijackers in pursuing their mission."

Abdullah was the ultimate fixer. He went above and beyond what a good Muslim would do for his brothers. He translated from English to Arabic for them. He helped them get driver's licenses and apply to flight schools.

After 9/11, there was a lot of smoke about Abdullah. Nearly three years before the attacks, he entered the United States through Canada on a B-2 visitor's visa. Once in San Diego, he sought asylum as a Somali refugee. At one point in his phony immigration tale, Abdullah used the name "Franco de Pollo," or Frank of Chicken. He was sticking it to the U.S. authorities.

Just one day before 9/11, Abdullah married a young girl called Wanda. It was an Islamic marriage that was eventually annulled. Immigration authorities said it smelled bad from the start. It looked like Abdullah knew what was coming. He was looking for imaginative ways to avoid deportation. And it's possible Abdullah left a child behind in the United States. Suffice it to say, we were not the only ones still interested in the Yemeni national.

An investigative journalist in San Diego, Kelly Thornton,

who is highly respected for her coverage of the hijackers after 9/11, told us that the FBI showed up on her doorstep when they learned she was in contact with Abdullah again. There appeared to be new information about a trip during which Abdullah was casing LAX, along with the hijacker Nawaf al-Hazmi and a third man.

After being deported, Abdullah was living in Yemen. Thornton still knew how to reach him. "I e-mailed him. And I was trying to run this by him and ask were you at LAX casing with Nawaf [al-Hazmi] and an unidentified man?

"I got a reply and basically he was pretty evasive. He didn't answer a lot of questions directly, and he said he doesn't remember the guy . . . [who] just happened to be tagging along."

Thornton thought the e-mail exchange was innocuous, but she still ran the information by the U.S. attorney's office. Thornton also understood there might be a video of the three men at the airport.

"Out of the blue, I was contacted by FBI agents in Los Angeles," Thornton said. "I thought it was very interesting, the timing of it. Years after 9/11, a couple of years after the e-mails had been exchanged, why the renewed interest in Mohdar?"

Thornton said the FBI agents who sat in her living room never explained why the e-mails were such a big deal. Nor did they explain the importance of the video that apparently showed Abdullah, al-Hazmi, and the unidentified man at LAX.

"I thought for certain he [Mohdar Abdullah] knew who that was. He was just being coy."

And significantly, Thornton said there was no doubt that Abdullah was the one who drove the newly arrived hijackers in February 2000 from LAX to San Diego, where they connected with the cleric. "I do believe they have them on video, and Mohdar himself told me he drove them [the two hijackers] from LAX."

After the attacks, Abdullah was held as a material witness and then thrown in a detention center on immigration charges. Sometime in the fall of 2003, he reportedly bragged to fellow inmates at a California detention center that he'd known that al-Hazmi and al-Mihdhar were planning a terrorist attack. Before that, he admitted to the FBI that he knew of the men's extremist thinking. While the prison rants could not be independently confirmed, the 9/11 Commission concluded that they were important, given his connection to the hijackers and also to al-Awlaki.

Significantly, the commission pushed hard to get access to Abdullah in 2003 and 2004, but to no avail. He was deported before Zelikow and others could question him. "At the time he was deported we were bothered by that," Zelikow told me. "It was puzzling to us that the United States would deport him to Yemen at that time."

"Because he had potentially so much information about the plot?" I asked.

"Yes, he had been interviewed before, but then there was some new evidence and some new questions that we wanted to put to him."

I pushed a little more. "Did you ever feel he was deported because an arrangement had been made with the Yemeni government in terms of intelligence sharing?"

"We did," Zelikow answered. "We could develop a lot of different hypotheses about why some of these people including Mohdar Abdullah were allowed to leave the United States and didn't find their way to Guantánamo. . . . The bottom line is that I don't know."

By January 2001, al-Awlaki had made his way from San Diego to the mosque in Falls Church, Virginia. The hijacker Nawaf al-Hazmi followed him. A third hijacker, Hani Hanjour, also came to al-Awlaki's mosque. Al-Mihdhar, who had come to the United States with al-Hazmi, left many months earlier because he was apparently homesick and wanted to see his first child. Investigators felt it was no accident that Abdullah accompanied al-Mihdhar to LAX before he left.

Then something extraordinary happened. It could not be another coincidence. In April 2001, Eyad al-Rababah, a Jordanian, came to the mosque in Falls Church, Virginia. He was looking for al-Awlaki. According to the 9/11 Commission Report, when the services were over, al-Rababah hooked up with al-Hazmi and Hanjour.

After the attacks, the Jordanian first told investigators he met the two hijackers at a store. He later admitted that the three connected at the mosque. He maintained it was a chance meeting.

A declassified Memorandum for the Record (MFR) from the 9/11 Commission Report shows that the FBI agent handling al-Rababah was immediately suspicious.

> Alrababah knew that the FBI was looking for him and went to FBI New Haven. His first "story" about meeting the hijackers at the 7-11 in Falls Church was a lie, and it took 10 months before he got his final version of the story, which SA [special agent] Bukowski characterizes as "90 percent" of the story. In the final version, Alrababah admitted to meeting the hijackers at the Dar al Hijrah [al-Awlaki's] mosque.
>
> SA Bukowski finds it suspicious that Alrababah would have had the meeting with Aulaqi and then turned around

and "ran into" the hijackers when there were 400 to 500 people at the mosque on Friday Prayers.

If Mohdar Abdullah, the Yemeni, was the West Coast facilitator for the hijackers, the Jordanian, al-Rababah, was the East Coast facilitator. After finding them a room at a friend's apartment in Alexandria, Virginia, al-Rababah eventually drove the men to Connecticut and New Jersey. On May 8, 2001, when al-Rababah showed up at their Virginia apartment, he found al-Hazmi and Hanjour with two "new friends," Ahmed al-Ghamdi and Majed Moqed. They were muscle hijackers who'd arrived at Dulles International Airport six days earlier.

"By what he [al-Rababah] claims as a coincidence, [he] meets Nawaf al-Hazmi and Hani Hanjour and then helps them not only in Northern Virginia but even [by] driving them to Connecticut and New Jersey," Zelikow explained.

The five men, led by al-Rababah, first drove to Fairfield, Connecticut. Al-Rababah said he eventually took the four hijackers to Paterson, New Jersey, to show them around. After a meal, the Jordanian said, he returned to Connecticut with the men and then never saw them again.

Within weeks, the hijackers rented a one-room apartment in Paterson. When their landlord showed up, he reported that six men were living there. They were all hijackers, including al-Hazmi's younger brother Salem. Eventually a seventh hijacker, Khalid al-Mihdhar, who knew al-Awlaki from San Diego, would join them.

The same MFR that details al-Rababah's "story" also claims the pressure was getting to him after 9/11. "Alrababah was not polygraphed. After some time in detention, he became incoherent and appeared to suffer some type of breakdown."

Based on our reporting, the evidence strongly suggested that al-Awlaki, the Yemeni Abdullah, and the Jordanian al-Rababah were part of a pre-9/11 support cell or support network. While the FBI questioned them all, the 9/11 Commission was developing leads of its own. Yet two of the suspects, Abdullah and al-Rababah, were deported before the 9/11 Commission investigators could get access to them. Did they know about 9/11 in advance or were Abdullah and al-Rababah simply following al-Awlaki's instructions? In addition, a declassified document from the 9/11 Commission report directly tied al-Awlaki and his mosque in Virginia to one of the 9/11 suspects. The document noted "the suspicious fact that the fax number for the Dar al-Hijra mosque was found with Ramzi Binalshibh in Germany. [Name redacted] emphasized the significance of a fax number being found—perhaps certain information needed to be transmitted that could not be discussed over a telephone."

As the interview with Zelikow wrapped, two issues stood out. First, Zelikow believed Khalid Sheikh Mohammed never came clean on potential U.S. contacts for the plot. "KSM was asked, many times, about whether there were contacts in the United States. And he always, from the reports we could read of those interrogations, he always seemed to blow smoke in answering questions like this."

Zelikow's description was ominous. Would this lead to a fundamental change in our understanding of the 9/11 plot? Were there not merely four cells of foreigner hijackers? Was there actually a fifth, domestic cell lying in wait to help?

"Do you believe that Awlaki was part of a cell inside the United States that was designed to facilitate 9/11?" I asked.

"We don't know," Zelikow offered.

I pushed harder. "Is it possible?"

"We did not know. Of course, it's possible."

"Does the evidence support it?"

"In writing about Anwar al-Awlaki in our report, we said expressly that we were very suspicious of his role, possible role in the attack . . . so that clearly says that we were entertaining the hypothesis."

"If there was a cell within the United States, that would completely change the way that we look at 9/11." I put the possibility to Zelikow. I hoped he would explain more.

"If you were able to prove that Anwar al-Awlaki had been part of al Qaeda and had been a sympathizer and was part of a support network for the 9/11 attacks, that opens up a whole series of additional questions, not only about al-Awlaki. . . . It would open up questions too about all the things that the captured 9/11 participants didn't tell us."

And here's the kicker: the information about al-Awlaki's return to the United States in 2002, the arrest warrant for passport fraud, the decision to rescind the warrant on the same day he reentered the United States, al-Awlaki's appearance in a high-profile FBI investigation—none of it was shared with the 9/11 Commission.

Zelikow and another high-level commission member said they could not remember the al-Awlaki documents. It was not the kind of information they would forget. Having reviewed the arrest warrant, a legal source on the commission said the extraordinary timing of al-Awlaki's return to the United States and the FBI connection demanded further investigation.

I would later argue, based on interviews with two senior members of the joint congressional inquiry, that the information was likely withheld from the commission and from Congress. The FBI has never publicly explained why one of its agents,

Wade Ammerman, told customs agents at JFK to let the cleric enter the United States on October 10, 2002, even though the warrant for his arrest on passport fraud was still active.

The FBI wanted the cleric in the country, but why?

The 9/11 Commission Report states clearly that FBI agent Ammerman was interviewed on October 16, 2003, just over one year after the cleric mysteriously returned to the United States, and after the bewildering decision to pull the arrest warrant. Yet it appears Ammerman did not flag these incidents to investigators.

It was such a glaring omission that after our *Fox News Reporting* special aired, Republican congressman Frank Wolf of Virginia, who sat on the powerful House Appropriations Committee, wrote to the FBI director demanding an explanation:

> I am deeply concerned about a recent report that the Federal Bureau of Investigation (FBI) ordered notorious al Qaeda recruiter Anwar Aulaqi be released from detention at Kennedy Airport in October 2002, allowing him to re-enter the United States with impunity, despite an outstanding warrant for his arrest. The questionable events surrounding the return of Aulaqi to the U.S. then and the subsequent dismissal of his outstanding warrant merit greater attention and transparency.
>
> This matter is particularly timely given Aulaqi's recent emergence as a leader of al Qaeda in the Arabian Peninsula (AQAP) and his recruitment of alleged terrorists Major Nidal Hasan, Umar Farouk Abdulmutullab, and Faisal Shahzad.
>
> What if he had been tried and convicted and sentenced to a prison term and had been prevented from many of his terrorist activities over the last decade? Could history have been

changed with regard to the attack on Fort Hood, Texas, the killing of the U.S. Army recruiter in Little Rock, Arkansas, the attempted Christmas Day bombing, and the attempted bombing of Times Square earlier this month?

The letter was initially met with silence by the Justice Department and the FBI. One month after it was sent, I went to a news conference on mortgage fraud because I knew Attorney General Eric Holder and FBI director Robert Mueller would be there.

As I asked my question of the FBI director, whom I have covered for nine years and whom I respect, I felt like the skunk at the picnic. "Mr. Director, why was it in October 2002 that FBI agents told customs to allow Anwar al-Awlaki into the U.S. and to hold him no longer at customs when there was still an active warrant for his arrest?"

It was awkward as Mueller stepped to the microphone. "I'm not familiar with the facts that you're raising. We'll have to get back to you on that, it does not ring true to me, but again, I'd have to look into the factual scenario you're positing."

We heard nothing from the FBI until October 2010, when our Freedom of Information request came through. In the spring, we'd asked for the intelligence memo that had been written about al-Awlaki on October 8, 2002, just two days before he reentered the United States.

The documents came direct to our senior executive producer, Pamela Browne. Pam had worked at every high-profile broadcast network newsmagazine. Pam was the one who found Brian Weidner. The former FBI agent explained the Bureau's chain of command. He took us inside the decisions that allowed al-Awlaki to slip mysteriously through the net.

Over the years, I'd developed a lot of respect for Pam. She was one of the few executive producers who'd earned the title. Pam was relentless in pursuit of the facts. And the best part of all—she wasn't afraid to get her hands dirty.

When the documents arrived via FedEx, we concluded that the bureaucrats were flipping us the bird. The FBI FOIA attorneys sent us twenty-seven pages of blankness. The Bureau cited national security and an executive order—most likely the warrantless wiretapping program. It was their way of saying we should butt out of the FBI's business.

The FBI was not the only government body throwing up roadblocks. In a lengthy statement, having refused our investigative team access to the U.S. attorney in Colorado who pulled the al-Awlaki warrant, the Justice Department insisted that al-Awlaki's reentry in October 2002 and the decision to pull the warrant were a coincidence.

The six-hundred-plus-word statement blamed bureaucrats at the Social Security Administration for forcing the U.S. attorney to pull the warrant: "The Social Security Administration would testify only that Awlaki was entitled to a Social Security number, that the number was valid, and that their records indicated that he corrected his place of birth."

So why did it appear that the U.S. government was bending over backward to claim al-Awlaki corrected the lie on his Social Security application? Anyone who has tangled with the federal bureaucracy knows there is no such thing as an easy fix.

Given my limited experience with the Social Security Administration, I wondered if correcting the record was really that easy. I spoke to three current and former Social Security investigators who poured cold water on the Justice Department claims. Two sources, with direct knowledge of al-Awlaki's file, said there was no correction of the record. The cleric had simply generated more inconsistent paperwork in his file when he applied, in 1996, for a replacement card as an American citizen born in New Mexico. Six years earlier, in 1990, al-Awlaki claimed to be a foreign student born in Yemen. The Social Security sources, who spoke with me because they didn't like being dumped on, said correcting the record required a formal mea culpa by al-Awlaki. And that never happened.

Congressman Frank Wolf also found the Justice Department's tale unbelievable. "Please provide all documentation that justifies the department's position that individuals [are] allowed to provide knowingly false information to the Social Security Administration and State Department and later 'correct it,' without penalty, as occurred in this case," he wrote.

And there was another problem for the Justice Department. The elaborate statement said that as a "matter of law or ethics" the U.S. attorney's office in Colorado could not pursue the case. Justice Department officials seemed to claim that al-Awlaki's American citizenship allowed him to flout the law once again. "As a U.S. citizen, Awlaki was entitled to the Social Security number and the renewal of his passport."

As Fox's senior media counsel, Carlotta Cassidy, would say, these guys didn't seem to understand the law. Carlotta pushed hard through the Freedom of Information Act to get the al-Awlaki documents from the FBI. She also got her hands on a decision by California's Ninth Circuit that further undermined the Justice Department's position.

The *Hart* case was powerful in its simplicity. In 2002, just before the U.S. attorney in Colorado pulled the warrant, the court ruled that you can't lie on a passport application, regardless of whether the information is material to the application.

Diplomatic Security agent Ray Fournier, who pinned al-Awlaki on passport fraud, briefed himself on the *Hart* decision before he met with David Gaouette, the U.S. attorney in Colorado. You recall that Gaouette summoned Fournier and another Diplomatic Security agent for a meeting in Denver two days before al-Awlaki reentered the United States. The bottom line: their hard work was for nothing.

When he raised the *Hart* case, Fournier said, Gaouette dismissed it. "He really didn't want to hear about it. He was not interested in the results of the Ninth Circuit decision," Fournier told me.

When I asked how that could be, Fournier speculated that other pressures were weighing on Gaouette. "Well, I think that he may have had other factors that he was considering. He expressed some concern that we were . . . the application of law was somehow different for Anwar Awlaki. And also he mentioned that he was concerned that we were going to—we the Bureau of Diplomatic Security—were going to use this Ninth Circuit decision to go after anyone . . . [and] bring droves of passport fraud cases into his circuit."

Fournier said that he and the other Diplomatic Security agent tried to reassure Gaouette that they wouldn't use the *Hart* decision to go after every illegal alien in Colorado. But no amount of convincing was enough. Less than seventy-two hours after Fournier left the meeting in Denver, the warrant was vacated.

I asked the obvious question. "So you are saying the U.S. attorney did not understand that your job was to go out and get a holding charge on this guy?"

For Fournier and other hardworking agents it was a sore point. "Apparently not."

Given the bizarre timing of al-Awlaki's return to the United

States, and all the documents connected to his return, Zelikow suggested Capitol Hill could help. "Subpoena power . . . I want to see everything in this time frame that you have," Zelikow said, describing how the FBI should be approached.

"And that's what Congress could do?" I asked.

"Yes," Zelikow said.

While the Bureau was apparently blocking information, new documents came to me from an unexpected source. While only two pages long, the FBI interview summary showed that al-Awlaki was taken to the Pentagon as part of the military's outreach to the moderate Muslim community in the immediate aftermath of 9/11.

A current Defense Department employee flagged the incident. Gail (I've chosen not to include her last name) came forward after the Fort Hood shooting. The media coverage of Major Hasan's e-mail relationship with al-Awlaki raised the cleric's profile. The DOD employee recognized the name immediately.

The first time I read the documents in a San Diego hotel room, I felt a chill. Al-Awlaki touring the Pentagon was like a criminal returning to the scene of the crime. The cleric had connections to three of the five hijackers on Flight 77. I imagined al-Awlaki walking the halls on the way to his lunch and smiling slyly as he quietly marveled at the destruction.

The documents state that Gail saw al-Awlaki speak at an apartment complex, "the Watergate at Landmark in Alexandria, Virginia." She told investigators that the international population at the Watergate "caused the Alexandria Police Department to provide extra protection as a possible target of a future terrorist attack."

After 9/11, the residents at the Watergate had dinners in the community room. One of those invited to speak was the "Imam of the Fairfax Mosque." "While she [Gail] arrived late she recalls being impressed by this Imam. He condemned Al Qaeda and the terrorist attacks. During his talk, he was 'harassed' by members of the audience and suffered it well. [Gail] was so impressed with this Imam's performance that she mentioned it to her boss," the interview summary read.

The investigators from the FBI and the Army Criminal Investigation Command summarized Gail's interview. She told them that getting the cleric in for lunch at the Pentagon was not a hard sell. "At that period in time the Secretary of the Army . . . was eager to have a presentation from a moderate Muslim."

The cursory background research on the cleric "found his writings to be as moderate as the presentation." The vetting process was described as minimal. "Virtually all she [Gail] knows of Aulaqi came from 'a friend,'" the documents continue. "Who may have obtained this information from another friend."

The FBI summary gets worse: "He was considered to be an 'up and coming' member of the Islamic community. . . . Aulaqi was invited to and attended a luncheon at the Pentagon in the Secretary of the Army's Office of Government Counsel." A Defense Department employee "escorted Aulaqi from the Metro up to the office for the luncheon."

After his Pentagon lunch, Gail told investigators that she believed al-Awlaki went on his Hajj and never returned to the United States. Later, Gail reported reading stories in the *Washington Post* that portrayed al-Awlaki as a radical cleric. Asked to speculate on whether the cleric was playing Defense Department officials for fools, Gail "proffered that Aulaqi is 'either a good liar or later something happened.'"

Asked if she had anything else to add, Gail said: "When

Aulaqi was at the Pentagon a chaplain approached Aulaqi stating that the Army suffered from a shortage of Korans and asked him if he might be able to provide some." After the cleric departed, the chaplain was counseled that "he had engaged in an unethical solicitation. The subject of . . . [the] post luncheon email[s] to Aulaqi was to inform him not to feel pressured or obliged to provide the Army with Korans."

We gave the Army nearly a week to respond. We wanted to know how al-Awlaki was vetted, who was at the lunch, and whether there were photos to memorialize the event. When there was still no response, we contacted Tommy White, who was the secretary of the Army at the time. He said he had no recollection of the event. "If there was a luncheon at the Office of Government Counsel, I would not necessarily be there," White said. When he asked for more detail on the cleric, and I explained it was the same American on the CIA's kill or capture list, White offered: "I definitely was not there. I would have remembered it. I do not recall being there."

The Army's spokesman called once the story went up on the Web. Apparently, the lunch was not an Army event. It was an Office of the Secretary of Defense (OSD) event. In those days, the OSD was Rumsfeld territory. "The Army has found no evidence that the Army either sponsored or participated in the event described in this report," spokesman Thomas Collins said in a statement. Collins also noted that the FBI document referred to the "Office of Government Counsel" but should have read "Office of General Counsel."

A spokesman for the OSD said no one believed al-Awlaki was a terrorist at the time. But when it was pointed out that the cleric was interviewed at least four times by the FBI in the first week after 9/11, the conversation came to an abrupt close.

A former high-ranking FBI agent, who was working counterterrorism after the attacks, was not surprised by the lunch.
He said there was tremendous "arrogance" about the vetting
process at the Pentagon. "They vetted people politically and
showed indifference toward the security and intelligence advice
of others," the former agent said.

Through a FOIA request, Fox's investigative team sought
more information about al-Awlaki's lunch. While we asked for
all "e-mails, letters or other communications . . . photographs or
video taken at the luncheon," only one document was produced
by Pentagon lawyers.

I laid the three-page e-mail out on my desk. While most of
the names were redacted, I could still see that more than sev-
enty people were copied on the invitation, including William J.
Haynes II. At the time, Haynes was the General Counsel, or
the chief legal officer, for the Defense Department.

At the very least, the documents showed that al-Awlaki was
in the United States as late as February 11, 2002. The lunch was
scheduled, at the cleric's request, a week earlier, on February 5.

Given the growing threat from al-Awlaki's group in Yemen,
reading the e-mail, sent January 24, 2002, was like stepping
into the twilight zone.

```
>Subject: Luncheon Speaker - Islam and Middle Eastern politics and
culture - February 5th - RESPONSE DATE - 1/31
>Importance:  High
>
>Hi everyone,
>
>   Remember our luncheon series?  Although this luncheon is not part
of that series, I have been able to obtain a speaker who can talk to
us on whichever of the above topics we would like, or give us a taste
of each, and to take questions.  Mr. Haynes has no objections to our
going forward with this project, but his schedule is too hectic to
commit at this time.  We probably need to narrow the topic to allow
for the short time at a luncheon.
```

>
>Anwar Awlaki is the Imam at Dar Al-Hijrah in Falls Church, Va, which
is one of the largest Islamic Centers in the United States. He is
currently working on his PhD in Human Resource Development at George
Washington University, received a Master of Education Leadership from
San Diego State University and his BS in Civil Engineering from
Colorado State University. He completed Islamic Studies in Yemen. He
has been doing extensive public speaking on the above topics,
especially since the events on September 11. Mr. Nihad Awad,
President of the Counsel of American-Islamic Relations has also
expressed interest in attending. Mr. Amr Moussa, the Secretary
General of the Arab League, will be in D.C. on February 4th and 5th,
although I don't think that our luncheon will have the clout to get
his attendance!
>
>I had the privilege of hearing one of Mr. Awlaki's presentations in
November and was impressed both by the extent of his knowledge and by
how he communicated that information and handled a hostile element in
the audience. I particularly liked how he addressed how the average
Middle Eastern person perceives the United States and his views on the
international media.
>
>I have reserved one of the executive dining rooms for February 5th,
which is the date he preferred, from 12:00 to 1:30. He will be
leaving for an extensive period of time on February 11th. We will
need a minimum attendance of 15 to get those rooms. Unfortunately, we
all have to eat the same thing and the food has to be served to get
one of those rooms. Assuming that sandwiches will be the easiest
thing to get consensus on, here are the selections:
>
>Smoked turkey
>Roast Beef
>Smoked Ham
>East side West side (beef, turkey and bacon on marbled rye)
Vegetarian
>- the chef will create something special for vegetarians
>
>It will come with a salad and beverage. The cost will range between
$14 to $15, depending on how many attend. If you are interested in
attending, please let me know the following ASAP:
>
>1. Your sandwich choice (remember majority rules) - if I am wrong
about a sandwich and you want to try for consensus on a hot chicken,
beef, pasta, seafood or salad, please let me know. Most of the others
will have additional expense.
>2. The time, if 12-1:30 is not the best
>
>I need a firm number and money by 1/31. My room is 3D941. Sorry for
the short notice, but we had several delays along the way!
>
>Thanks for your consideration - I think you'll enjoy it if you come.
He is very informative and this is certainly a hot topic that we would
all like to learn a little more about.
>
>

I took off my reading glasses and shook my head. Pentagon lawyers thought a lunch for an "up and coming" so-called moderate Muslim should include smoked ham and bacon? No wonder things went bad.

And once again, the cleric was padding his résumé. Our research showed that al-Awlaki never got his degrees from George Washington University or San Diego State.

The Defense Department was not the only bureaucracy under pressure. Remember the al-Awlaki audiotape with a message for the American people? The Middle Eastern source that hooked me up, Yemeni journalist and terrorism expert Abdul Elah Hider Shaea, was now in a Yemeni prison. Yemeni media said he was arrested at his home in the capital, Sana'a. Among the government's accusations: he was affiliated with al Qaeda, he was a spokesman for the group, and, significantly, he had "relations" with al-Awlaki. Shaea was later convicted on terrorism charges. One media report noted that he was picked up after he appeared on Al Jazeera TV with critical views of the Yemeni government and its handling of al Qaeda. It sounded like payback to me. For now, the pipeline to al-Awlaki was plugged.

While an alleged confidant of al-Awlaki was sitting in prison, others came to the cleric's aid. In the summer of 2010, the ACLU filed suit against the U.S. government on behalf of al-Awlaki's father, Nasser, who was also in Yemen. The civil rights group argued that al-Awlaki's name should be pulled from the CIA's kill or capture list because Yemen was not a war zone and there was no imminent threat. The ACLU said the order amounted to a mandate for the "extrajudicial killing" of a U.S. citizen by his own government.

In a federal court filing, the Obama administration fired back that the ACLU had no business poking its nose into the al-Awlaki matter. Justice Department lawyers cited the state secrets privilege. They claimed the case threatened to expose sources and methods.

As of this writing, I don't know which rabbit hole the case will eventually go down. But once again it seemed al-Awlaki's American citizenship was the ultimate shield protecting him.

. . .

If al-Awlaki was al Qaeda's American star, the old guard at Guantánamo was still languishing at the Navy base. By the fall of 2010, more than half of the detainees were like al-Awlaki. They came from Yemen, and no solution for solving Guantánamo's Yemeni problem was on the horizon.

For the 9/11 families we've had the privilege of meeting— the retired school nurse Mary Novotny, Brian and Melissa Long, and Gordon Haberman—there was no significant movement on their case until April 2011.

On the same day that President Obama announced his bid for re-election in 2012, Attorney General Eric Holder said that Khalid Sheikh Mohammed and his four co-defendants would now be tried—not only in military court, but also at Guantánamo Bay. Holder blamed Congress for blocking the funding for a civilian trial in lower Manhattan: "I know this case in a way that members of Congress do not. I've looked at the files. I've spoken to the prosecutors. I know the tactical concerns that have to go into this decision. So, do I know better than them? Yes."

In a brief e-mail, a former New York City fireman thanked me for staying with their story. He was relieved that the lives of the jumpers, a reference to those trapped in the Twin Towers who leapt to their deaths, were worth more than the rights of the terrorists.

If I had one regret, it was that our team never filmed an interview with FBI agent Wade Ammerman. I was the only one who had any contact with him. He directed all of my questions to FBI headquarters in Washington, D.C. He would not talk without his higher-ups' permission. It never came.

As a courtesy, because I don't like blindsiding folks in my reporting even if they never cooperate, I gave Ammerman a heads-up that our show was airing. Ammerman was the FBI agent who asked customs to open a file on al-Awlaki in the summer of 2002. Customs agent David Kane said it was a lookout. When the cleric entered the United States, he would be detained and arrested because of Fournier's outstanding warrant for passport fraud. But sometime between the summer of 2002, when the file was opened, and October of that same year, something changed. When al-Awlaki was detained at JFK International Airport on October 10, 2002, Ammerman told customs to let him go even though the warrant for al-Awlaki's arrest was still active.

Neither the FBI nor my law enforcement contacts ever challenged our conclusion that the Bureau was trying to cultivate al-Awlaki as a human intelligence asset. Or at the very least, the Bureau wanted to track the cleric after he entered the country.

I understood that Ammerman was not senior enough to call the shots on al-Awlaki, given the cleric's strong connections to the hijackers. The Bureau doesn't work that way. The clearance had to come from higher up.

Ammerman made only one comment to me. You can decide what it means. My notes were sketchy, but it went something like this: "I don't think anyone wants me talking 'bout what I was involved in."

Less than three weeks after Fox's special *The American Terrorist* was broadcast, the FBI leaked the first mug shot of Anwar al-Awlaki to the media. It was from a 1997 charge for soliciting prostitutes. The mug shot was not leaked to Fox.

Fox News Bureau

Washington, D.C.

November 5, 2010

1700 hours

"Catherine Herridge, call 6364."

The overhead paging system is sounding.

"Catherine, call 6364."

There is urgency to the call. The extension goes directly to the news desk. The editorial coordinator needs something confirmed, and fast.

A short time earlier, a lightning bolt had come across the news wires. It was an urgent alert. Al Qaeda in Yemen was claiming responsibility for two cargo bombs and the downing of a third cargo jet in Dubai.

I pick up the phone. As I talk to the editor on the news desk, I am multitasking. I open my e-mail and drop the lightning-bolt wire into the text. Next I type the address. Once again, it is the NEFA Foundation. "D. K. Draper"—I am talking softly as I type—"R. Sandee, and E. Kohlmann." Evan Kohlmann was the investigator we met in chapter 1 who first found Anwar al-Awlaki's statement praising the alleged Fort Hood shooter, Major Nidal Hasan, as a hero.

Within minutes, Evan replies. I open the Web link he's sent. It is a banner, commonly seen on the jihadist forums, with three photos. Two include cargo planes. The third picture shows the bomb.

Eight days earlier, on October 28, 2010, President Obama learned from his national security team that suspicious packages were bound for the United States. One package was intercepted at an airport in the United Kingdom and the other package was stopped in Dubai. A Saudi intelligence tip led investigators to both packages. The tip was described as specific—so specific that it led to the packages' tracking numbers.

They were shipped from Yemen and addressed to long-dead historical figures who had slaughtered Muslims. As the *New York Times* reported, one package was addressed to Diego Deza, whose cruelty to Muslims during the Spanish Inquisition was documented. The second package was sent to Reynald Krak, who was a French knight who killed Muslim pilgrims with abandon. Using these names was al Qaeda's equivalent of black humor. The bombs' senders figured or at least hoped that the packages would never reach their final destinations.

The bomb maker was infamous. Ibrahim Hassan al-Asiri was the handyman behind the bomb stuffed in Umar Farouk Abdulmutallab's underwear. He was also behind the so-called butt, or cavity, bomber who attempted to assassinate a Saudi prince in the summer of 2009.

Now, video of al-Asiri's lab was on my mind. Pamela Browne had flagged it months earlier. She had seen something in it that the rest of us had missed. Pamela knew instinctively that it needed a second look. A Saudi contact sent our team fresh video of the cavity bomber and the send-off by his brother, the bomb maker. The two men embraced, and at least one seemed to weep.

It made me stop and think. The bomb maker was willing to send his own brother, Abdullah Hassan Taleh al-Asiri, to a certain and horrible death. That is what a terrorist is made of. A White House that considers apologizing for the United States and its foreign policy would do well to remember it.

In the lab, the young brother is only hours or days away from his guts being blown across a room. He looks happy. On his left is a glass beaker. He holds a small object in his hand.

The object is shaped like a teardrop. This is the first time the picture is sharp enough to make out what looks like a hand grenade. The suicide bomber appears to be showing off the explosives that will kill him.

I pause and lean back in my chair. If you want to look inside the heart of the enemy, watch what he does to his own brother.

. . .

The printers, at least one from Hewlett-Packard, were carefully engineered. The toner cartridge was packed with the explosive PETN, the same explosive used in the underwear bomb. It is apparently al-Asiri's explosive of choice.

A senior U.S. counterterrorism official tells me the detonator did *not* rely on cell phone or satellite phone service. That resolves a puzzling question. At high altitudes or buried deep in the cargo hold, it would be impossible to get the signal necessary for detonation.

Long before we have a lot of detail about the bombs, investigators are entertaining a novel theory. The bombs are not meant for Chicago synagogues or Jewish community centers in the president's hometown. They are meant to blow up in the United States or in U.S. airspace.

This makes the most sense. We know that al Qaeda in Yemen, with the American cleric in its ranks, wants to go global. It is determined to make a name for itself. It is determined to hit the U.S. homeland. Bringing down a UPS or FedEx jet over the Atlantic is not its MO.

The source for the Saudi tip is intriguing too. My open-source contact, David, feels that a former Guantánamo detainee, and onetime leader within al Qaeda in Yemen, is the likely source.

Jabir Jubran Ali al-Fayfi was picked up in Yemen and transferred to the Saudis less than two months before the cargo bombs were loaded onto jets. The timing wasn't quite right. Al-Fayfi had been "off the battlefield" for several weeks. David and I conclude that he might be connected, but it was unlikely the Saudi national was the direct source.

It got me thinking. Except for al-Awlaki, most of the leadership of al Qaeda in Yemen were Saudi and former Guantánamo detainees. Like al-Fayfi, who was detainee number 188, they'd attended the Saudi "Betty Ford" clinic for terrorists, graduated, and returned to the battlefield. I thought the acronym SALY— for Saudi Arabians living in Yemen—was fitting. It was assuredly disrespectful and catchy.

As the story evolves, there is another unsettling development. We confirm a dry run in September. U.S. counterterrorism officials say the package was linked to a person with known al Qaeda connections. Its contents were innocuous—a bunch of religious books—but one investigator is disturbed by the destination.

A clue may be buried in al Qaeda's *Inspire* magazine, the second issue. I turn to page 51, where I find the Chicago skyline, including the John Hancock Building. When the Saudi intelligence tip came in, counterterrorism analysts connected the picture with the dry run. The red warning lights were blinking.

A former intelligence officer at the Transportation Security Administration drops an e-mail in my in-box. Bill Gaches is convinced that al Qaeda in Yemen was using the cargo Web tracking system on the dry run to calibrate the time of detonation. He says investigators will scrutinize the dry run to see whether the plotters tracked the package's travels by date, time, and place. "I would think they were timing this and perhaps they were able in fact to, with some precision, track where the package was and consequently wait until it got into U.S. airspace."

Nine days after the bombs were discovered, British police confirmed that the cargo bomb was set to go off early in the morning on Friday, October 29, 2010. "If the device had not been removed from the aircraft the activation could have occurred over the eastern seaboard of the U.S.," the British police statement said.

After the bombs were found, Homeland Security sent a cable warning that the plot might be linked to language schools in the Yemeni capital. It caught my attention immediately because the schools teach Arabic, often to English speakers. American jihadists were known to study there. It raised the very real possibility that Americans knew about the plot in advance.

It was a clever plot, another sign that al Qaeda and its affiliates were thinking out of the box.

As we took off our shoes at the airport, the terrorists were busy designing a bomb for the cargo hold on jets. Experts said 60 percent of the cargo heading into the United States from overseas was carried on passenger planes. It was more proof that after all these years, al Qaeda and its spawn were still obsessed with aviation. I imagined the 9/11 suspects at Guantánamo's Camp 7 would smile with approval.

While the plot was rooted in Yemen, U.S. intelligence anticipated that the American cleric played a role. He was rising through the ranks of al Qaeda in Yemen as an operational planner. He understood that cargo screening was one of our blind spots. To search every package would shut down the U.S. economy.

Only an American, I thought, could exploit our weaknesses so effectively. The danger was clear. The next wave of al Qaeda recruits, the American recruits, was already here. Like al-Awlaki, they were born here or raised here—an increasing number were naturalized citizens.

They were old enough to remember 9/11, yet they turned their backs on the nation that offered them hope and an education.

They spoke English. They blended into the crowd. They were the new gold standard for al Qaeda. The agent who knew the cleric best, former Diplomatic Security agent Ray Fournier, had one final thought. "We are in a war of survival," he wrote. "We can ill afford to clumsily apply our legal system and fail to prosecute facilitators of death such as Anwar Nasser Abdullah Aulaqi, who personifies the agenda of our enemy."

As I sat at my desk, surrounded by documents and old cups of coffee, I leafed through an internal Justice Department report one last time. A new homegrown plot with links to international terrorism was documented, on average, every two weeks.

I sat back in my chair. Would we be so lucky the next time?

EPILOGUE

Guantánamo Bay, Cuba

Latitude: 19 degrees 54 minutes north

Longitude: 75 degrees 9 minutes west

July 17, 2009

I t was a simple gesture. The yellow foolscap airplane glided silently across the military courtroom at Guantánamo Bay. It landed on the desk of Ali Abdul Aziz Ali—one of five 9/11 conspirators accused of murdering nearly three thousand Americans.

Ali has several aliases, including Ammar al-Baluchi. His pedigree is good for al Qaeda. His uncle is Khalid Sheikh Mohammed—who is also held at Guantánamo in the highly secretive Camp 7, where no journalist has ever been allowed to report by the U.S. government.

Al-Baluchi is accused of being a glorified travel agent for the 9/11 hijackers. He was the moneyman who funneled the cash from his base in the United Arab Emirates. He bought the plane tickets. He made the hotel reservations. He says he often did similar work to supplement his income. He claims he didn't know what was up.

But his family connections suggest otherwise. Al-Baluchi's cousin is Ramzi Yousef, who was convicted in 1997 for the first World Trade Center attack. It is well understood within intelligence circles that once al Qaeda picks a target, it will come back again and again, until the job is done. For Khalid Sheikh Mohammed, the World Trade Center was not only al Qaeda's obsession; it was—through his nephews al-Baluchi and Yousef—a family obsession.

Al-Baluchi picked up the paper plane from the defense table and opened it quickly. There appeared to be a message inside, and as al-Baluchi read it, he began to laugh. He laughed so hard it seemed like a grade school trick.

The plane had been thrown by Walid bin Attash, who was clearly in on the joke. I could see his long white robe, his customary attire for court, shaking as he leaned across his defense table. Five defense tables, one for each defendant, line the left side of the courtroom, which was custom-built for their trial.

Bin Attash is a small man from Yemen. According to his defense lawyers, his manners are impeccable. He once excused a member of the defense team, Navy lieutenant commander James Hatcher, from a hearing because he was getting married the same week. It became a running joke that the marriage was off to an exceptional start. It was blessed by God and by al Qaeda.

Hatcher was assigned to the case in March of 2008. He visited with his "client" at least once a month without fail. Hatcher put aside his personal feelings about his client and his alleged role in the attacks. The mission required it.

Bin Attash is not a household name, but his al Qaeda pedigree is well documented. He is sometimes referred to as "al Qaeda royalty" because his family and Osama bin Laden's family were friends.

With one leg lost in Afghanistan fighting the Northern Alliance more than a decade ago, Bin Attash has street cred. He has also been accused of laying the groundwork for the simultaneous suicide bombings of the U.S. embassies in Kenya and Tanzania in 1998 and the strike on the USS *Cole* in 2000, before conspiring in the 9/11 attacks.

Back in the Guantánamo courtroom, Bin Attash and al-Baluchi were laughing hard now. I was only twenty-five feet away, but I couldn't hear them through the reinforced glass. The military guards were moving us along because the court was transitioning from an open to a classified session. The journalists had to go.

Some days later, once I returned to Washington, D.C., a legal source explained that Bin Attash had written either the 9/11 flight numbers or the jet tail numbers inside the yellow foolscap airplane. My source was sketchy on the details because the information was relayed to him by a military guard who had apparently retrieved the paper plane.

The symbolism of the plane, and the flight numbers, in a military court laid bare the darkness in these men's souls. It flashed before me in an instant, and the realization made me feel physically sick. You don't see evil often, but when you do, there is no mistaking it.

Since, I have thought privately that every government official who makes a decision about these men's fate should spend a half hour in court with them. Better yet, five minutes in a Camp 7 cell would be sufficient. It would take only a second for their gut to tell them it's time to throw away the key.

ACKNOWLEDGMENTS

It's called the acknowledgments, but every writer knows it is much more than that. This is the part of the book that I've looked forward to the most. It is also the hardest to write.

A book starts as the writer's idea, but pretty soon you realize it takes a team to get it into print. It is with gratitude and humility that I am honored to thank the team behind *The Next Wave*.

Crown committed to the project before al Qaeda's American recruits made national headlines. I am especially grateful to publisher Tina Constable for her vision. She saw the merit of investigating al Qaeda 2.0 and the American cleric long before he and his group, al Qaeda in Yemen, were declared a greater threat than Osama bin Laden.

In Sean Desmond I found an editor who distilled a complex subject into five neat chapters. He instinctively knew when to let me run with the details and when it was time to rein me in.

Thank you for your clarity and sound judgment. Thank you for the honor of working with you.

It has also been my pleasure to work with editorial assistant Stephanie Chan, production manager Norman Watkins, production editor Mark Birkey, and jacket designer David Tran.

For publicist Campbell Wharton and for Meredith McGinniss of marketing, thank you for showcasing the team's hard work.

This book would never have appeared without my book agent, the brilliant Mel Berger at William Morris Endeavor Entertainment. Thank you, Mel, for believing in my ability. Thank you for identifying a compelling narrative.

Having listened to so many tales from the road, my TV agent, Henry Reisch, also at WME, knew I had a book in me. Thank you for trusting me to deliver. Thank you for opening the door to the world of TV and books when we first met fifteen years ago.

Ralph Peters is a friend and a mentor. Ralph has more than twenty-five books to his name, and his advice to this first-time author was graciously accepted. His only request was that one day I would help someone else.

Charles Krauthammer honors me with his friendship. His interest in and support for my reporting from Guantánamo gave me the courage to push ahead against fierce opposition.

Greta Van Susteren has supported my reporting, and most of all she has shown tremendous kindness to our family. Thank you for shining a bright light on the issue of transplantation.

Paul Friedman gave me my first job in TV and introduced me to ABC News London. Thank you for the chance to learn from journalists who covered Vietnam, the Marine Barracks bombing, and the first Gulf War. No newsroom has ever compared.

Like all big projects, there are many people behind the scenes who deserve credit: Carl Kropf, George Little, Marie Harf, Paul Gimigliano, Mark Mansfield, Brian Hale, Kelly Nantel, Brandon Alvarez-Montgomery, Michael Birmingham, Ross Feinstein, Dean Boyd, Andrew Ames, Richard Kolko, Paul Bresson, Jason Pack, Katy Montgomery, Chad Sweet, Marc Raimondi, Kevin Bishop, Shane Wolfe, Kevin Gundersen, Kevin Fogarty, Daniel Scandling, Thomas Culligan, Jamal Ware, Dave Yonkman, Leslie Philips, Roger London, Ellen Howe, Payne Sterling, Greg Soule, Sean Smith, Matt Chandler, Joe Della-Vedova, J. D. Gordon, Vanessa Loftus, Tim Goldsmith, my friends in the Fox make-up department, and Daniel J. Wilkinson.

I owe a special thanks to Clark Kent Ervin of the Aspen Institute and investigative journalist Kelly Thornton, whose reporting took us inside the San Diego 9/11 support network.

Current and former administration officials gave their time, their analysis, and their firsthand accounts: Michael Hayden, Charlie Allen, Tom Ridge, Michael Chertoff, Janet Napolitano, Dale Meyerrose, Philip Zelikow, Michael Leiter, and Kip Hawley.

Former deputy commander of Joint Task Force Guantánamo, Gregory Zanetti, provided details about Khalid Sheikh Mohammed, including his obsessions with martyrdom and the media.

There are the investigators whose dedication to the mission often goes unrecognized: David Kane, Ray Fournier, Steve Schultz, Tony Shaffer, Chris Voss, Brian Weidner, G. I. Wilson, "Ally," "David," Daniel L., Paul K., Bill Gaches, the NEFA

Foundation, David Draper, Ron Sandee, and Evan Kohlmann, as well as Memri.org, including Richard Wachtel and Executive Director Steven Stalinsky.

Defense attorneys Edward MacMahon Jr., James Hatcher, and John Galligan were constant reminders of why America is a great nation. They put their personal feelings and politics aside to provide the best defense possible for their clients—some of the most hated men.

For the small but mighty Fox investigative team, our work stands for itself. The *Washington Post* called *The American Terrorist* an "explosive hour."

Pamela Browne is a shining star—one of the finest senior executive producers working today. She saw the importance of tracing al-Awlaki's American life within days of the Fort Hood shooting, on November 5, 2009.

Carlotta Cassidy, Cyd Upson, and Gregory Johnson are true professionals. Kristin Noyes and Steve Carlson sifted through old records and data to help our team identify and confirm critical information for our investigative timeline.

For the families of 9/11 and the USS *Cole*, thank you for trusting me with your story: Kirk Lippold, Gloria and John Clodfelter, Lee and Eunice Hanson, Brian and Melissa Long, Robert Reeg, Gordon Haberman, Hamilton Peterson, Alice Hoagland, Mary Novotny, and Debra Burlingame.

Debra deserves special recognition for her pursuit of justice on behalf of her brother and others.

Without the love and support of my parents, my sisters, my husband, and my children, I am nothing. And without them, the book would have remained another idea, tucked away in a drawer full of old notebooks. A special tip of the hat to my husband, J.D., because, from his secure base in the man cave, he supplied the comic relief.

Jennifer Murray reminds me every day what real friendship means. Researcher Martha M. Hurley improved the manuscript in ways I could not have accomplished myself.

Before I wrap up, I want to thank you, the reader, for giving me your time. I would never take it for granted. Now I need you to do something. Next time you see someone in uniform or if you know an agent, officer, or analyst working to keep our nation safe, simply thank him or her for serving.

NOTES

Prologue

The prologue is based on my firsthand account as well as my reporting notes for the Fox News Channel of the arraignment of Khalid Sheikh Mohammed and his four co-accused at Guantánamo Bay, June 5, 2008. "Guantánamo General Tells Story of the Hidden Khalid Sheikh Mohammed," www.foxnews.com, December 16, 2008. Interview Janet Hamlin, October 23, 2010. Interview Commander J. D. Gordon, October 12, 2010.

Information on Americans with alleged ties to international terrorist groups was drawn from a Justice Department background briefing document. Additional information was gathered from the U.S. attorney's office in the Carlos Bledsoe case and from U.S. Department of Justice press releases for Hosam Smadi and Betim Kaziu.

The change in al Qaeda's recruitment strategy comes from several sources: Dennis C. Blair's "Annual Threat Assessment of the US Intelligence Community for the Senate Select Committee on Intelligence," delivered February 2, 2010; congressional testimony by CIA director Leon

Panetta, February 2, 2010; and an interview with Charlie Allen for *Fox News Reporting: The American Terrorist.*

Chapter 1: Made in the USA

This chapter is based on interviews with former CIA officer Charlie Allen and former Diplomatic Security agent Ray Fournier for *Fox News Reporting: The American Terrorist.* Separately, I interviewed former CIA director Michael Hayden, defense attorney John Galligan, and the former commander of the USS *Cole* Kirk Lippold. It also relies on my reporting and contemporaneous notes for the Fox News Channel, beginning with the Fort Hood shooting, from November 5, 2009, through October 30, 2010.

To understand al-Awlaki's life leading up to and including the 2001 attacks, I have drawn on the 9/11 Commission Report; NYPD Special Analysis Anwar al-Awlaki, December 1, 2009; and documents from www .intelwire.com, including an FBI report from September 26, 2001. This chapter also draws extensively from research by the NEFA Foundation (www.nefafoundation.org), including "Anwar al Awlaki: Nidal Hassan Did the Right Thing," November 9, 2009; "Target America: The Fort Dix Plot," January 2008; "Oussama Kassir Expert Report and PowerPoint," by Evan Kohlmann, May 14, 2009; Video Transcript of Former Gitmo Detainees Swearing Allegiance to Al-Qaida in Yemen, February 1, 2009, by Evan Kohlmann; "Salutations to al-Shabab of Somalia," December 21, 2008; and "Al-Qaida Claims Attempted Assassination of Saudi Prince Nayef," August 31, 2009.

I also drew on these published sources: McClatchy Newspapers, "Neighbors Describe Fort Hood Suspect as Kind, Generous," November 6, 2009; "Suspect Was to Deploy to Afghanistan," *Army Times,* November 6, 2009; "Army Tests Sole-Killer Theory as Details Emerge," www .nytimes.com, November 6, 2009; Associated Press, "Fort Hood Suspect Said Goodbyes Before Attack," November 6, 2009; "Exclusive Video: Surveillance Video of Hasan," CNN, November 6, 2009; "Fort Hood Gunman Gave Signals Before His Rampage," www.nytimes.com, November 8, 2009; "Exclusive / Ray Suarez: My Post-9/11 Interview with Anwar al-Awlaki," www.pbs.org, November 11, 2009; "Understanding Ramadan: The Muslim Month of Fasting," with Imam Anwar al-Awlaki, www.washington post.com, November 19, 2001; "Fort Hood Shooting: Texas Army Killer

Linked to September 11 Terrorists," www.telegraph.co.uk, November 7, 2009; "5 Men Are Convicted in Plot on Fort Dix," www.nytimes.com, December 22, 2008; "The Powerful Online Voice of Jihad," www.thestar.com, October 18, 2009; "The Secret Sharer," interview with Michael Leiter of the NCTC, *Columbia, the Magazine of Columbia University,* September 2009; "Closing Guantanamo Fades as a Priority," www.nytimes.com, June 25, 2010; U.S. Department of State, Background Note: Yemen; "Charges Detail Road to Terror for 20 in U.S.," www.nytimes.com, November 23, 2009; "Somali Investigation Timeline," www.startribune.com, August 5, 2010; "Al Qaeda–Linked American Terrorist Unveiled, as Charges Await Him in U.S.," www.foxnews.com, September 4, 2009; "The Making of a Minnesota Suicide Bomber," www.startribune.com, May 3, 2009; "Pennsylvania Woman Indicted in Plot to Recruit Violent Jihadist Fighters and to Commit Murder Overseas," www.justice.gov, March 9, 2010; Department of Justice Press Release, "Women from Colorado and Pennsylvania Charged with Terrorism Violations in Superseding Indictment," April 2, 2010; "Mother of 'Jihad Jamie' Describes Daughter as 'Lonely and Insecure,'" www.foxnews.com, March 15, 2010; "White House Adviser Briefed in October on Underwear Bomb Technique," www.newsweek.com, January 2, 2010; "New al-Qaeda 'Body Bombs' That Can Beat Airport Security Are Alarming Terror Experts," www.telegraph.co.uk, October 3, 2009; "Qaeda 'Ass'assin," www.nypost.com, September 30, 2009.

Chapter 2: The Digital Jihadist

This chapter is drawn from interviews with Charlie Allen, Jim Moore (who asked that his real name not be used for security reasons), former FBI agent Brian Weidner, and the executive director of the 9/11 Commission, Philip Zelikow, for *Fox News Reporting: The American Terrorist.* It also draws on the 9/11 Commission Report.

Al-Awlaki's criminal record for soliciting prostitutes in San Diego and Washington, D.C., as well as loitering around a San Diego school comes from a Memorandum for the Record (MFR) for the 9/11 Commission, November 18, 2003. Al-Bayoumi "roughhousing" hijackers, MFR for the 9/11 Commission, October 18, 2003, obtained from www.intelwire.com.

This chapter also relies on information from the National Intelligence

Estimate, July 2007, Key Judgments, "The Terrorist Threat to the US Homeland," and the NEFA Foundation, "44 Ways to Support Jihad," www .nefafoundation.org. I have also drawn on documents, videos, and reports from the Middle East Media Research Institute (MEMRI), www.memri .org, including an interview with Omar Hammami, known as "Amriki," by Al Jazeera 2007; al-Shabaab release "Amriki," training and transcript, March 31, 2009; Hammami addressing President Obama, July 9, 2009; "Festival for the Children of the Martyrs"; and *Inspire* magazine and reaction from the jihadist forums, "Release of Al-Qaeda's New English-Language Magazine Ends in Jihadi Web Disaster," July 1, 2010.

Case information comes from the following government sources: Carlos Bledsoe, DOJ press releases, June 2, 2010, and June 3, 2010; FBI press release, June 5, 2010; Walter Barry Bujol, U.S. attorney's office, the Southern District of Texas, June 3, 2010; Mohammed Alessa and Carlos Almonte, DOJ press release, June 6, 2010, and criminal complaint.

Congressional testimony on the emerging homegrown threat is drawn from the testimony of Brian Michael Jenkins of the Rand Corporation before the Senate Homeland Security Committee, November 19, 2009; and "Al Qaeda in Yemen and Somalia: A Ticking Time Bomb," Report to the Senate Committee on Foreign Relations, January 21, 2010.

I also drew on the following published sources: Council on Foreign Relations, "Somalia's High Stakes Power Struggle," August 7, 2006; Associated Press, "N.J. Men Accused in Terror Plot Appear in Court," June 7, 2010; "US Missiles in Yemen, Amnesty Says," www.upi.com, June 7, 2010; "Alleged Fort Hood Shooter Frequented Local Strip Club," www.foxnews.com, November 9, 2009; "Agents of Terror Leave Their Mark on Sin City," SFGate.com, October 4, 2001; "Madrid Bombers Get Long Sentences," BBC News, October 31, 2007; "Seeking Terror's Causes, Europe Looks Within," www.nytimes.com, September 11, 2007; "Al-Qaida Launches English-Language E-zine," www.upi.com, July 1, 2010; "Al-Qaeda Launches *Inspire*, Its First English Language Magazine," *Vanity Fair*, July 1, 2010; "N.C. Congresswoman Calls for American to Be Stripped of Citizenship over Al Qaeda Website," www.foxnews.com, July 20, 2010; "Bombing in London; Terror Threat Subway Suspect Is Shot to Death by London Police," www.nytimes.com, July 23, 2005; "Subway and Bus Blasts in London Kill at Least 37," www.nytimes.com,

July 8, 2005; "Bombings in London: The Investigation," www.nytimes
.com, July 27, 2005; "U.S. Citizen Believed to Be Writing for al Qaeda
Website, Source Says," CNN, July 18, 2010.

Chapter 3: Slipping Through the Net

This chapter is based on interviews with former Diplomatic Security agent
Ray Fournier, former customs agent David Kane, defense attorney Edward
MacMahon Jr., author Paul Sperry, and former FBI agent Brian Weidner.

For this project, I was granted rare access to analysts at the CIA who
cover Pakistan, Afghanistan, the Arabian Peninsula, Somalia, and North
Africa. I was also given rare access to members of the radicalization unit at
the National Counterterrorism Center; I give grateful thanks to both the
CIA and the NCTC for shedding light on their important work since 9/11.
Separately, a senior U.S. counterterrorism official agreed to provide context
for my reporting on the condition that the source not be identified.

Several documents make up the backbone of this chapter. They include
the arrest warrant for Anwar al-Awlaki issued in Colorado in June 2002;
court documents to pull back the warrant in October 2002; the TECS log,
first obtained by author Paul Sperry (www.sperryfiles.com); FBI memo,
September 26, 2001, obtained by www.intelwire.com; NYPD Special
Analysis Anwar al-Awlaki, December 2009; and court filings provided by
MacMahon in the Ali al-Timimi case.

I also drew on the following published reports: "Anacostia Naval
Station," www.globalsecurity.org; "Va. Muslim Spiritual Leader Gets
Life," www.washingtonpost.com, July 13, 2005; *United States vs. Hart,*
Openjurist.org, March 15, 2002; Justice Department Response to Fox News
Regarding Colorado 2002 Awlaki Matter, May 21, 2010; Reporters Com-
mittee for Freedom of the Press, "Material Witness Label Keeps Detainees
In, Media Out," Fall 2002; "FBI Sets Up Shop in Yemen," www.time.com,
August 2003; "Al-Amoudi Brought to Justice," *Washington Times,* August 7,
2004; DOJ release, "US Announces Plea in Terrorism Financing Case," July 30,
2004; "Officer Failed to Warn C.I.A. Before Attack," www.nytimes
.com, October 19, 2010; "Najibullah Zazi," Times Topics, *New York Times,*
December 18, 2010; "Pakistani Involvement in the Mumbai Attacks," www
.time.com, December 4, 2008; "Intel Chief: Errors Made in Bomb Case,"

www.cbsnews.com, January 20, 2010; "The 9/11 Memorials You Haven't Seen," Liveshots Blogs, www.foxnews.com, September 10, 2010; "Anwar al-Awlaki Had 'Direct Operational' Role in Attempted Christmas Day Bombing," www.foxnewsinsider.com, June 30, 2010; TECS database "electronic databases," www.gao.gov; "UK 2006 Liquid Explosives Plot Trial Overview," www.tsa.gov, September 7, 2009.

Chapter 4: Justice Delayed

This chapter is based on my firsthand accounts for the Fox News Channel of Major Nidal Hasan's court appearance at Fort Hood, Texas, June 1, 2010; of the military commission hearings from July 2008 through the fall of 2010 at Guantánamo Bay; and of tours of detention camps 4, 5, and 6 and the Camp Iguana demonstration. It also includes my reporting on the Uighurs and their transfer from Guantánamo Bay to Bermuda in June 2009.

The chapter also draws on interviews with Commander J. D. Gordon, military commissions spokesman Joe DellaVedova, Senator Lindsey Graham, Cully Stimson of the Heritage Foundation, Steven Emerson of the Investigative Project, defense attorney John Galligan, and former FBI agent Chris Voss. Forensic psychologist Marc Sageman was interviewed for *Fox News Reporting: The American Terrorist.* I also relied on Michael Leiter's question-and-answer session at the Aspen Security Forum, June 2010.

Other sources included the 9/11 Commission Report and the Senate Intelligence Committee Report on the Attempted Christmas Day Bombing, May 18, 2010.

E-mail relating to Guantánamo Bay and decisions regarding access was provided to me by a source who asked to remain confidential.

I also drew on these published sources: Ft. Hood PDF, "Fort Hood Quick Facts," "personnel," www.goarmy.com; "Obama Attends Memorial Service for Victims of Fort Hood Shooting," www.guardian.co.uk, November 10, 2009; "Hasan Makes First Court Appearance," www.kvue.com, June 1, 2010; "Hearing for Fort Hood Shooting Suspect Delayed," www .statesman.com, June 1, 2010; "Evidence Hearing Delayed for Accused Fort Hood Killer," www.aolnews.com, October 12, 2010; "Obama Orders Secret Prisons and Detention Camps Closed," www.nytimes.com, January 22, 2009; "Heartfelt Thanks," www.jtfgtmo.southcom.mil, July 20, 2009; "U.S. Says Seeking 60-Day Delay in Guantanamo Trials," www

.reuters.com, September 16, 2009; "Obama Endorses Military Commissions for Guantanamo Detainees," www.csmonitor.com, October 29, 2009; "Departments of Justice and Defense Announce Forum Decisions for Ten Guantanamo Bay Detainees," www.justice.gov, November 13, 2009; "Judges Reject Evidence in Gitmo Cases," www.law.com, August 16, 2010; "The September 11 Defendants," www.humanrightsfirst.com; "U.S. Likely to Seek Death Penalty for Sept. 11 Terror Suspects," www.foxnews.com, November 13, 2009; "Obama Administration Takes Several Wrong Paths in Dealing with Terrorism," www.washingtonpost.com, January 31, 2010; "Briefing by White House Press Secretary Robert Gibbs," www.white house.gov, February 12, 2010; Senate Select Committee on Intelligence, "Unclassified Executive Summary of the Committee Report on the Attempted Terrorist Attack on Northwest Flight 253," May 18, 2010; "Khadr Has Right to Burial in Canada: Son," www.cbc.ca, January 24, 2004; "Canadian at Guantanamo Pleads Guilty to War Crimes," www.miamiherald .com, October 25, 2010; Associated Press, "Some Issues Still Blocking Sept. 11 Trial, Holder Says," July 11, 2010; "Top 9/11 Suspects to Plead Guilty," BBC News, December 8, 2008; "Try Sept. 11 Suspects in U.S. District Court for Guantanamo," www.washingtonpost.com, July 16, 2010; "Khalid Sheikh Mohammed Will Be Held in Military Prison Without a Trial Indefinitely: Report," www.nydailynews.com, November 13, 2010; "U.S. Approves Targeted Killing of American Cleric," www.nytimes.com, April 6, 2010.

Chapter 5: Guess Who's Coming to Lunch

This chapter is based on interviews with Michael Hayden, Dale Meyerrose, Lieutenant Colonel Tony Shaffer, and former ranking member of the House Intelligence Committee Republican congressman Pete Hoekstra. I also interviewed Charlie Allen and journalist Kelly Thornton as part of an upcoming *Fox News Reporting* special.

Nearly a decade after former Diplomatic Security agent Ray Fournier secured an arrest warrant for Anwar al-Awlaki in 2002, Fournier provided much-needed context on the failure of the FBI to detain the cleric, who has now become one of the U.S. government's most wanted terrorists.

I also obtained through a confidential source an FBI summary that came to light as a result of the Fort Hood investigation. The two-page document details al-Awlaki's lunch at the Pentagon as part of the military's outreach to moderate Muslims in the immediate aftermath of 9/11. Through a FOIA request, Fox News obtained an internal e-mail revealing the guest list, the menu, and the scope of al-Awlaki's proposed discussion.

It would seem no chapter is complete without reference to the 9/11 Commission Report and to research provided by the NEFA Foundation, www.nefafoundation.org, whose analysts identified al Qaeda in Yemen's claim of responsibility for the printer cargo bombs in October 2010.

I also drew on the following published reports: Associated Press, "Report: New Al Qaeda Leader Knows U.S. Well," August 6, 2010; "Al-Qaida Mastermind Rose Using American Hustle," www.npr.org, October 11, 2010; "Most Wanted Terrorists Adnan G. El Shukrijumah," www.fbi.gov; "Qaeda Leader Indicated in New York Subway Plot," www.nytimes.com, July 7, 2010; "Congressional Inquiry: How Did Shahzad Become a U.S. Citizen?" www.cbsnews.com, May 6, 2010; "Government's Memorandum in Connection with the Sentencing of Faisal Shahzad," September 29, 2010; "Faisal Shahzad," Times Topics, www.nytimes.com, October 5, 2010; Trac Reports, "Department of Justice Program Categories Covering Terrorism"; "Homeland Security Secretary Michael Chertoff Announces Six-Point Agenda for Department of Homeland Security," www.dhs.gov, July 13, 2005; "Lashkar-e-Taiba," Times Topics, www.nytimes.com, June 16, 2010; "Chicago Resident David Coleman Headley Pleads Guilty to Role in India and Denmark Terrorism Conspiracies, Admits Conducting Surveillance for Lashkar e Tayyiba," www.fbi.gov, March 18, 2010; "Somali Militants 'Behind' Kampala World Cup Blasts," BBC News, July 12, 2010; "Exclusive: Witnesses in Defense Dept. Report Suggest Cover-up of 9/11 Findings," www.foxnews.com, October 4, 2010; Associated Press, "Weldon: Atta Papers Destroyed on Orders," September 16, 2005; Agence France Press, "Georgia Targeted in Cyber Attack," August 12, 2008; "Harris Corporation Names Major General Dale W. Meyerrose," www.harris.com, January 12, 2009; Government Computer News, "Ridge Criticizes Sluggish Implementation of Security Technologies," www.americansecuritychallenge.com, September 23, 2010; Mohdar Abdullah's immigration history, indictment on immigration fraud, June 28, 2002; Nasser Arrabyee, "Hit and Run Style of Al Qaeda in Yemen," September 28, 2010, and "Yemeni Journalist Put on Trial over Terror Charges," October 26, 2010; "Targeted Killings," www.aclu.org, April 28, 2010;

"Earlier Flight May Have Been Dry Run for Plotters," www.nytimes
.com, November 1, 2010; Pamela Browne, senior executive producer, Fox
News video al Qaeda in Yemen bomb maker and lab; "Cargo Bomb Plot,"
Times Topics, www.nytimes.com, October 2010; *Inspire* magazine, volume 2; Associated Press, "Experts: Passenger Planes Also at Risk from
Cargo," October 31, 2010; "Exclusive: Al Qaeda Leader Dined at the Pentagon Just Months After 9/11," www.foxnews.com, October 20, 2010.

Epilogue

The epilogue is based on my firsthand account of one of the last military
court appearances of the 9/11 suspects before Attorney General Holder's
announcement in November 2009 that he intended to send the men to federal criminal court. Only three of the five men bothered to come; Khalid
Sheikh Mohammed was among the no-shows.

I also interviewed Lieutenant Colonel James E. Hatcher, the attorney
for Walid bin Attash. Background information on the detainees is drawn
from the 9/11 Commission Report; "Ammar al-Baluchi" biography, www
.defense.gov; and the detainees' biographies at "Announcements Detainee
Biographies," www.dni.gov, September 6, 2006.

I also drew on the following published report: "Profiling the Terrorists," www.time.com, September 6, 2006.

INDEX

About the Author

Catherine Herridge is an award-winning TV correspondent who has worked for the Fox News Channel as well as ABC News. Now based in Washington, D.C., covering intelligence, homeland security, and the Justice Department, Herridge has reported from Afghanistan, Iraq, Israel, Qatar, the former Yugoslavia, Northern Ireland, and New York City on 9/11.

Herridge and Fox's investigative team traveled across the U.S. and to Yemen to complete a six-month investigation into the American-born cleric Anwar al-Awlaki, who is linked to three of the 9/11 hijackers, the massacre at Fort Hood, the attempted Christmas Day bombing, and the cargo printer bomb plot in October 2010.

Fox News Reporting: The American Terrorist concluded that critical information—including court documents about al-Awlaki's mysterious return to the U.S. in October 2002—was withheld from the 9/11 Commission. Fox's reporting, which prompted letters from Capitol Hill, was described by the *Washington Post* as "an explosive hour."

Herridge has also traveled to Guantánamo Bay, where she reported on the detention operations and the military commissions, including the arraignment of Khalid Sheikh Mohammed and his four co-conspirators in 2008. Herridge went to Harvard College and the Columbia School of Journalism. This is her first book.